DEATH
AND
FUTURE LIFE

—

DISCOVERY PUBLISHER

For the French edition:
2015, Discovery Publisher

For the English edition:
©2016, Discovery Publisher

Author: Maurice Magre
Translator: Nathalie Glowaty
Editor: Edward Adwill
Editor in Chief: Adriano Lucca

DISCOVERY PUBLISHER

616 Corporate Way
Valley Cottage, New York, 10989
www.discoverypublisher.com
books@discoverypublisher.com
facebook.com/DiscoveryPublisher
twitter.com/DiscoveryPB

New York • Tokyo • Paris • Hong Kong

TABLE OF CONTENTS

DEATH
AND
FUTURE LIFE

—

Preface

I aspire to make men happy by understanding death. I aspire to set back the limited prospects of their future, until billions of centuries. I aspire to multiply the inner treasure of each. I want the patient to stop fearing, the old man to think of his future youth, the agonizing to thank because of the next light, and families to sang with joy during funeral ceremonies.

I know the vanity of my aim. I know that human beings carry with them their initial doubt with the fervor of the one who carries a Blessed Sacrament during a procession.

I know that when it comes to the subtle life of the afterlife, one demands instantly material proofs of this existence which has no matter. I know that man is like a blind man to whom one describes in vain the beautiful landscapes which are before his eyes and who only believes in the parcel of substance touched by his hand. That is why I will present no decisive proof, no forceful argument for the unlimited joy I promise, I will offer no beverage of certainty, no nectar of mathematical demonstration, I will provide nothing, only the testimony of a sincere man.

I am not writing for scholars hallucinated by the light of their science, nor for the ecclesiastics who crush the brass cap of dogma, or for the ones who call themselves oculists and who lost themselves in the void of their secrets. I am not writing for those who are indifferent, for those that the everyday enjoyment of life has made short-sighted, nor for the stupid ones who cherish their ignorance, or for the too intelligent who know everything. I am not writing for those who are respectful of old customs and of ancient thoughts, for the fathers, for preachers of salons, churches or café, for the glorifiers of modern life or even life itself. I am not writing for the defenders of order, nor for those who wants to destroy it. I am not writing for the rich because the word does not cross the obstacle of possession. I am not writing for the poor who only aspire to eat and sleep more. I am writing for the others and they are maybe more of them.

And perhaps they will not believe me. It is the gesture of the messenger who gives value to the message. One knows the meaning of the words by the mouth which will pronounce them. I have not clothed myself with the immaculate robe and with the hieroglyphic miter of a venerable indicator of death. For failing to appear important, it is possible that one doubts me. Yet I will pass on the message.

Those who will hear it for the first time will undoubtedly say that they have known it at all times and that it is old as the world. It is at his age, indeed, that one recognizes the excellence of a truth. Pure as a diamond, polished like the rock crystal, fluid as the solar morning light, these are the virtues of this truth. It lies in the heart of every man, but it has to be extracted from the hard earth of ignorance. It lay dormant in me and it awakened. I do not know at what time of my life the seed was filed, or whether it was by the hand of a sower, or by a cosmic stream responsible for fertilizing souls. But this seed is hatched. It grew up, it is like a tree which opens its branches, which shades and protects me.

I am sitting under the tree of the joyful certainty. The knowledge of death is the greatest wisdom of life. Several Sphinx smiled at me and talked to me benevolently. Others, which are still on the heights might come down to me.

I learned in what way the river of evil took its source and I could safely contemplate its French Riviera waters where pass blind fish and dead bodies with sirens busts. I discovered that I cherished in me without knowing the monstrous dragon of selfishness. I wanted it out and I realized that this was impossible and that it was powerful and beautiful. I was sad at first, then I thought that the fate of monsters was to perish sooner or later, heart pierced by a loving thought.

Through the beatitude of understanding, I saw that on the balance of destiny, every happiness had an exact counterweight of intelligence. I learned that earth's poison came from the rot of hypocrisy and that the old Satan was always beside us, dressed as a good man. With joy, I heard around me the snap of rotten societies near to collapse. I tasted an endless happiness while feeling my soul expand, seeing the stars a thousand times more numerous than before and the multiplication of solar systems in spaces which will be granted to me to pass. I owe all this to the knowledge of death.

Praise be to death which when one meditates on it, divest of its funeral rags, drops its bones of parade in order to take the body of beauty and the face of hope.

From the necessity to study death

I was surprised that I had been capable to go through life without being concerned by the knowledge of death. I was surprised of having so much carelessness, or rather indifference. Thus, loved ones had ceased to live beside me and I had done nothing to know how the essence of their beings had transformed! I had let them move away in the opacity of shadows without seeking to understand the color thread of sun that could have united me to them.

I was also surprised by the small number of people who had a similar concern to mine.

I noticed that, generally speaking, individuals could be divided into two classes, depending on whether they were turned towards the afterlife or whether they had of the afterlife an instinctive fear and were content with phenomena that stand to reason.

I like those who think of death. The death of those they loved and their own death. They form a small family whose members recognize each other by the first words exchanged with them. They are neither smarter nor more virtuous in the narrow sense of the word. As I have observed it for myself, the study of death develops certain qualities that one might equally call moral than immoral, but which are the sign of a certain decrease of selfishness. One cannot say that they are more likely to make good deeds. They are not less than the others attached to pleasure and sometimes they are even more. They look like men who would have once breathed the scent of a goddess and could not forget it.

But one should not look for the secret of death because of the terror one feels about it. It will not reveal itself to you.

The terror inspired by death is the result of the lowest superstition. Many people begin to fear the beings they loved and that they have lost, from the moment they come to shed the smallest opportunity of being impressive. It is neither by curiosity nor by fear, but by love for others that it is necessary to take a look from the side of death. And then an unexpected phenomenon takes place. One sees very far in this unexplored area and the more one looks with a sincere heart, the more the view is unlimited.

Thus, it happened to me, by fixing in meditation the problem of death, to see emerge in me truths that were unknown to me and that contradicted everything I had believed until then. No proof confirmed them. However, they were of an unquestionable character and it would have seemed laughable to me to doubt them.

***

There was one day when it appeared to me with clarity that I had to discover this magical key which is the secret of death.

I considered that suffering was widespread on earth in a proportion infinitely broader than joy. What was then called joy of life was only an instinctive joy to breath, eat, and satisfy sexual instincts. But as soon as intelligence manifested, pity appeared at the same time. One could measure the moral value of someone to his capacity of pity. It would not be possible for a truly superior man, that is to say totally pitiful, to bear the existence. It is because our life represented a lower order, and it took place in the shallows of creation, in a sort of cosmic hell. It was essential to get out of it.

I wanted to have an immediate revelation on the way of starting, to be set in few hours on the human destiny. Yet, there is no book where this revelation is clearly enunciated. There is undoubtedly no man who can give it orally. It is furthermore mysterious. Perhaps it is a vital law of the universal order, one of these strange laws that govern us, that man should not know his fate after death. Fortified with the certainty of a better life, all those who suffer down here would hasten to commit suicide, and nature in its love of life, did not want this extinction contrary to its purpose.

Religious dogmas have an infantile character and look like imageries whose aim is to scare or make someone laugh. If one asks those who teach these dogmas they say that they are sacred in their simplicity, that it is necessary to honor their naïve symbols, but they add in a low voice that they are not to be taken to the letter. Great western philosophers have wanted to establish systems so great that they lost themselves in labyrinths of abstraction and that one gets lost after them. They are always tormented by the shadow of their religion. Nothing can be awaited from their philosophy for the knowledge of death.

The knowledge of death comes out slowly from the study one makes from it and doubts by which one is seized during this study. It is necessary to doubt a lot in order to believe. Many men have written books where they have accumulated documents, comparisons and the affirmations of other researchers and in these books is reflected the constant will not to discover the truth. Their reading is more useful that those of the publications of sincere faith. I believed for a long time that I had found nothing in their writings, and I doubted with the skeptics. As for me in the middle of the ocean of those books, as this sailor who, believing himself lost very far from the coast, through the fog, saw when he despaired, that he arrived in the calm waters of the harbor.

It is not the faith that must be found, but the certainty of its reason. Just as one reaches the knowledge of any science in an evening's work, one cannot perceive lives from the afterlife and the transformations of the man during these lives without a long preparation.

After many readings, and many meditations on different beliefs, I only saw that since the beginning of the world, wisest men and the shrewdest of humanity had reached the same conclusions. Saints, mystics, a great number of philosophers, despite the mold of their religion, had agreed on a certain number of points, the essential points. This agreement came most of the time without having communicated between them. With different details, they all made of the future life a similar description. This description was found in the discrepancies of visionaries and of those who claimed to see by a gift of clairvoyance. It was also found if one looked carefully under the vast puerilities of primitive religions.

Yet, when I had realized this impressive concordance, I saw that it was supported by something powerful and irrevocable which was my inner

certainty. These essential points on the future life of man and his possibilities in the afterlife, these points to which had believed the best,
smarter and more reliable men, they were in me as dormant truths. These
truths had slept under my ignorance and under my doubt. They awoke
by making contact with the feeling of their existence that the greatest intellects than mine had before me. A new faculty had appeared in
my soul that allowed me to recognize truths from lies. I had connected
with my intuition to the chain of the wise who passionately scrutinized
the problem of death.

All man of good faith, following the same stages that I followed, will
be able to reach the same certainty touching the same truths. I will indicate these stages by apologizing myself of quoting myself too often
as an example. But an experience can only be well understood if one
indicates the personal reactions of the one who made it. I wish mine
provides to those who will follow it, the same benefits of the soul.

One should not expect too much from these benefits although they are
vast. They do not alleviate the portion of the element of pain in which
everyone must live. The disease is no less painful, the forgetfulness of
those we love, less heartbreaking. It is even more harder since it prac-
tices against an element to which one recognizes an eternal character.
But we know now the quality of the current that carries you. A limit
is given to its hope. We know that the passage of death does not bring
the reign endured of justice. We know that the same laws, with their
transcendent lack of morality continue to perform for the dead as for
the living. We can prepare to use them to avoid pain, not to lose the
ones we love, to become more perfect by love. In view of the rule of life,
one come to understand the mystery hidden in the most admirable and
most dangerous of the words : life is beautiful!

It is with the magic of these four syllables that men deceive themselves,
limiting their horizons. The knowledge of death makes understand the
beauty and its relation to life. There is beauty whenever the inner spirit
appears under the movement of forms. Life is beautiful indeed. But
it is not only the superficial life where the setting suns throw fugitive
lightning, where beautiful female faces light up for a moment, it is the

immense life, the one which precede and the one that follow ours. The more we get away from the terrestrial world the more we get closer to the world of the mind. It is through the door of death that one comes to beauty.

The silence of the founders of religion

There has been great founders of religion, wise men who by going through life have provoked stirs of peoples. Several have been deified, either because the perfection of their life characterized them as divines, or because they invoked themselves in their speech a direct filiation with God.

Those, I said to myself first, have owned the secrets of the afterlife. They have not revealed them to everyone. They are not red in the sacred books of their cult or in the abstracts of their interviews. But perhaps they have revealed them secretly to their disciples. A truth of a universal order and of a so powerful interest is difficult to keep to oneself.

It had to be voiced under some symbolic form. It should let its light pierce in the corner of some conversation. It is important to know in all their details, the life of God's envoys, of the masters of illumination and to know the words only by sunset, under some oriental tree with silent leafs as the mystery of the soul, they have told to young men dressed in white and eager to learn.

The teachings of the great masters stored for me a disillusion.

— When one ignores what life is, how one is supposed to know what death is, said with a powerful logic the Chinese Confucius. Buddha repeated continuously that his doctrine was only a method to escape the suffering of successive lives and that it was not necessary to take care of metaphysics. The ideas of Pythagoras were surrounded by numbers as much of the small mysterious creatures which defended its entrance. By his constant interrogations, Socrates in the Athens's crossroads, seemed to have wanted to instruct himself, instead of instructing the others. Jesus had spoken of a kingdom of God that is reached after death, but he had indicated no precise data about this kingdom, only the absolute impossibility for a rich to get there, which, in some cases, could contain some injustice. Mahomet's paradise, on the contrary, offered certainties of enjoyment so precise, that it was unlikely as a child's dream.

All the prophets seemed to have known nothing exactly of what happens to humans after death.

And another disappointment, more bitter perhaps than my unsatisfied desire of knowledge, came from the legendary history of prophets.

I add faith to the legend. Anecdotes, character traits, spiking stories transmitted from mouth to mouth seem to me the best certainty of history. I found them more authenticity than the events which reality has been scientifically established. I do not doubt the existence of the legendary characters and if a word full of substance was able to come down through the centuries, I believe it has every chance of being true. It is therefore the voice itself of the prophets I heard, by following the story of their life, these are their real actions that took place in front of me and I felt as deeply their nature by the effort of intuition that I could feel those of the living men who were moving around me.

Whoever had moralized a third of humanity and printed in the soul of the Chinese, for twenty-five centuries, the love of rituals and the cult of ancestors, Confucius had given in his life the example of a wretched ambition. He had not ceased to have as ideal to become the minister of a king. He placed above all filial piety and himself never visited the tomb of his father. He flattered ridiculously the powerful to the point that he gave to his son, when he was born, the name Carp, because the sovereign of the country had sent him that day a fish of this species. He saw once a father hitting his son with a stick. He reproached to this child of receiving stoically the blows instead of fleeing. The stick of the father was heavy and could have caused death. Therefore, he had lacked of filial piety by risking his father to become a murderer. At the time of his death he told his disciples that since no one has told him the direction of any state, it means that there is on earth no smart prince and one of his last concern is to remember he descends from the emperors of the Inn dynasty, assertion that was based on nothing, and that was a sign of excessive pride.

Buddha's life is a sequence of poetic and moral events and it forms the most beautiful story that has been written since the beginning of the world. However, by reading the stories of Buddha's interviews with the kings of Magadha, seeing his extreme prudence toward the authorities of his time, his respect for the social order, I could not help myself to prefer the formidable independence of Jesus. Buddha was the chief of a great congregation of monks. Of this congregation were excluded slaves, those who had a position in the royal government in order not to disrupt the organization of the temporal authority and more unfairly, those who had an ulcer or a boil, one-eyed persons, eunuchs and those who had on their bodies traces of flagellation.

Yet, Buddha received as a disciple Angulimala the bandit, who wore around his neck a necklace made with the fingers of those he had killed. When the king of Magadha who murdered his father, comes to ask him if such action may have adverse consequences for his future life, he answers ambiguously and do not wither the parricide because he is king. If one is free from the yoke of the gods, one must also know how to free oneself from the yoke of men.

Socrates' death, as told by Plato, fills the soul with amazement. However, it must be recognized that the contempt of death is a virtue that is found in many ordinary men. Personal ideas that I made myself from the highest virtues do not allow these higher virtues to be practiced in conjunction with those required of a soldier. Yet, Socrates was a courageous hoplite and if he did not exercise command, he was renowned among his comrades for his fearlessness. He had to cross the body of the enemies of his homeland by throwing javelins or by hitting them with an acute lance during hand-to-hand combats where men loose conscious of himself, sees his native piety faint and allows himself to be dominated by the love to kill.

The physiognomist seer Zopyros, recognized on the face of Socrates signs of a powerful sensuality and when the disciples of the wise protested upon hearing this statement, Socrates said: what Zopyros has seen is true.

A certain violence and to some extent, a taste of vengeance surprised me even more in Jesus' life. That is was one reproaches the most to one-self, what appears to be the lower part of human nature, one would not want to meet in the great models of humanity. Seized by fury, he shouts:

— Snakes, brood of vipers, how will you avoid being condemned to the fire of Hell!

He chases with whips the sellers out of the Temple. There must have been there many small harmless traders who supported their families from the product of their trading talismans or objects of worship and who did not deserve this brutal aggression. He brought out the demons of the body of a madman and he passed them into a herd of swine that he sends to the sea to drown. I pity the innocent swine and the owner of the swine, unfairly dispossessed.

A woman came to him, says the Gospel, with an alabaster vase full of perfume of great price she spread on his head when he was at the table. Those who are with him regret with reason the price of the perfume that could have been sold in order to give money to poor people. But him, he is pleased with this homage which yet obviously belongs to the kingdom of earth.

Muhammad, whose religion is, of all, the one which now makes most of the proselytes, disconcerted me even more. The fact that he had, in the last years of his life, ten women instead of four that tolerates the Koran, that he has dyed in black his eyebrows and his nails in red with henna, that did not scandalize me. But this clever leader of the warlike tribe of Medina who defeated the Jewish tribe of Banu Qurayza, gave the order to massacre the hundred prisoners he made and sells women and children as slaves. In another victory, he takes hold of a Nadr ibn al-Harith, literate man who once in Mecca, had contradicted him. He thought for three days, then he put him to death. He takes advantage of a quarrel between the inhabitants of Medina and the Jews to remove his personal enemies. There are two things that delight me, he said, women and perfumes. Once he saw the beautiful Zeinab, the wife of his adoptive son and he likes her perfume. His adoptive son must divorce right away to give him the possession of this new woman.

I apologize for having brought back so few light of the journey I made with those who held the light and who have shown prodigal of it to all. I have yet accompanied them faithfully. I watched the smile on their lips to see if the irony was associated with wisdom. I admired the sometimes theatrical fold of their coat, happy that a certain beauty of attitude is not incompatible with great compassion.

I apologize for having been disappointed of what that compassion was not more heartbreaking. I would have liked they could not bear the pain of humanity, and that they die of pity instead of drinking the hemlock or climb on the cross. I apologize for a requirement that is justified by nothing. Maybe were there sublime hidden virtues where I thought I saw weaknesses? But perhaps the weaknesses are inherent to the sublime virtues and sermons on the mountains would have no price if the path of the peaks was not bristling with rocks on which it falls? I apologize for distinguishing among all spiritual leaders, what seems to me more shocking than a vice, pride.

It is perhaps madness to place so high modesty and wanting to find it in characters almost divine. I apologize for not having been able to hear or not to have understood them. None of them has revealed to me the secret they claimed to know. Perhaps they simply did not know it or they only had of it a half certainty. I had to look for it elsewhere, where it is located, in the compact matter of doctrines, in the darkness of philosophies, under the clouds of particular revelations.

For the invisible silver chain of the true word has not ceased to circulate across the ages and through it, by conveying to each another, men avid of knowledge have been united to one another. These are the men who have not sought fame and remained most often obscure, who are the true spiritual seed of humanity.

I apologize for wanting to bind myself to this less glorious fraternity, which, far from the path of religions, has found the narrow path that leads to the knowledge of death.

The world and the moon of the Hindus

The philosophy of India is like a mysterious forest as complex as all the planets of the creation. It is so punctuated by repetitions, incomprehensible words, invocations to numerous Gods that it is difficult to penetrate it.

In this forest, there are the primitive Vedas which ascend up to the sky as stone columns. There is the vast expanse of the Ramayana and of the Mahabharata. There are three baskets of the Tripitaka with copses of sermons and bushes of sung rules. There are ponds of still water where flourish the lotus of good faith and the lotus of mercy. One says to oneself that it will never be possible to embrace and penetrate everything. But if one does not let oneself frighten by the Mantras, the Jatakas, the Udanas and the severe laws of Manu, one founds at the end under the mountain of vegetations, the small and clear source where one can quench his thirst for knowledge.

In the ancient Brahmanical doctrine, the individual soul of the man is identical to the universal soul. This individual soul transmigrates through a series of lives which are painful. It frees from pain "only by its joining to the universal soul, joining realized by taking conscience of its identity with it, what is Moksa, the salvation"*.

According to the Vedic hymns and the Brahmanas, the deceased passes through an interim period of one year during which it can haunt the places where it had lived. This period can be compared to the one, of the same term, that set the Jewish religion for the separation of the double. It is the reason which forbids families to visit the tombstone of the dead during the period of one year. Folktales of India as those of other peoples are full of stories of ghosts.

Philosophers of India did not put in doubt the survival of the soul. It has always been an absolute fact, considered as indisputable. This cer-

* OLTRAMARE, *Histoire des idées théosophiques dans l'Inde.*

tainty must have come from a primitive legacy of knowledge, dating from the period when the tradition was still oral. Since ancient times, they had fixed the destiny of the soul after death.

There are two paths, the one of the Fathers and the one of the Gods. After death, some souls go to the moon and others to the sun. Naturally, the words sun and moon have to be heard symbolically. On the primitive data were established numerous theories which discussed a multitude of sects. He philosophy of India which has reached its highest point of height in the thirteenth century of our era with Shankara and his school, is based on the ancient wisdom that is found in the primitive writings and it is, in short, only an explanation and a comment of these writings.

At the moment of death, the subtle elements of the being are concentrated in the heart, then they rise and it is by the top of the head that the soul leaves the body it ceases to live in.

The ordinary man, "the man who do not know, says Shankara, entering these subtle elements which are the seed of the future body, to emigrate, accompanied by his previous works and will incorporate once again".

This is the destiny of the vulgar, even though this vulgar forms the vast majority of creatures. These are the works, the Karma which determines the future life of man who has taken the path of the Fathers and reaches the world of the moon. This one is enchained to the chain of transmigrations. He will come back on earth after a passage by a series of different states that the symbolic of texts designates by ether, air and rain.

Virtuous men and more advanced in the knowledge take the path of Gods and reach the world of the sun. There, they enjoy a relative immortality which extends to one or more cosmic periods. But at some point of the time, they will have to regain the path of transmigrations.

There is a permanent salvation only by the liberation which allows to escape to the world of forms.

"The liberation can only be achieved through a direct perception of the identity of the individual being with the universal self. It will be neither by Yoga (physical training), nor by Sankhya (speculative philosophy), neither by the practice of religious ceremonies, nor by the pure science*".

The one who has reached the liberation by an inner knowledge, very different from the one of the books, has exceeded the world of Gods, he came out of the current of forms, he enjoys the eternal beatitude, he identified himself to the universal soul.

The reform of the Brahmanical doctrines by the Buddha was only the input of a method to liberate oneself and remove the return of the future births and future deaths. The Buddha, as all great spiritual reformers, revealed a part of what has to remain hidden. This is what suggested that he was excluded from the Agartha and never obtained the highest initiation.

However, he has always refused to clearly explain what happens to the man after death. He voluntarily said that this knowledge was useless for the liberation and he undoubtedly thought that it was likely to delay it. There cannot be other reasons to his silence. If indeed, one has the certainty of the states of beatitude, otherwise eternal, at least of a long duration, after death, one will feel the desire to enjoy these states and the final liberation will be put aside for later.

But in his interviews with his disciples, he has revealed the certainties he possessed.

The Buddha admitted that it was possible to be reincarnated in several orders of creatures which were the animals, the demons, men and different categories of Gods. At the moment of the separation of the soul from the body, the power of the desire hurries the soul in a living germ which then develops in an organism, producing consciousness. The future birth is determined by the quality of the desires one has developed in one's life. The more the desires are of a rude nature the lower is the world to which one is attracted to. The more one has developed a high and spiritual consciousness, the more the organism where the soul projected itself will offer new means of development. But the soul cannot choose deliberately. Death takes away its choice faculty. There is an unconscious addition of its possibilities which rush it in the world of which it became worthy of, among the beings who are its peers.

---

* Shankara.

It is logical that actions that one has accomplished count less then, than the intentions that one has sustained internally. The pan of the determining balance tilts under the weight of the true inner faculties. One benefits from the outcome of its actions only to the extent that the actions are the symbols of true intentions and virtues.

This law is less rigorous than it appears at first.

Everyone visits the kingdom where its affinities call, which is more in accordance with himself. Everyone has the opportunity to fulfill its aspirations. Only this possibility is an obligation. The man with exclusively bestial tendencies is reborn in a world of beasts. We will see that this idea that goes against our western ways of thinking, is found in all the great Greek philosophers.

What seems more striking in the teaching of the Buddha, is the omnipotence, magical in a way, it attributes to desire. If one reaches by the detachment of terrestrial things and the love of knowledge, the world of Gods and if one enjoys there the wonders of thought, even after millions of centuries, it would suffice of only one material desire to throw the ancient god in a lower world. There, he will be dragged from one desire to another, and the ancient course with the same difficulties and the same sufferings, will restart.

Thus the Buddha taught that all the modes of incarnation, even the most subtle, were the causes of pain. There were between them only differences in term of period. Brahma himself would die one day. It was necessary to surpass the world of the pure joy and of the ideal speculation by the destruction of all desire, even the spiritual desire, and achieve the superconscious elation of Nirvana.

The Ka of the Egyptians

The one who wants to fathom the old Egyptian religion is greeted by a silent figure, several thousand years old, anointed with balms and salts, soaked in natron, tight with bandages and wearing a metal beetle on the place where his heart beat. This creature from beyond the grave, this still living creature, does not need to hand him the papyrus covered with hieroglyphics it carries under his left arm to teach him what the oldest science in the world knew of death. The papyrus, despite the research of all Maspero and of all Lepsius , keeps in fact its indecipherable enigma. But it is enough for the mummy to be present in its narrow sarcophagus. It testifies after several thousand years, a love of life so prodigious that those who felt it wanted to prolong after death that life, even weakened.

Reduce physical death! Give the being the opportunity to enjoy even after death, of the beloved matter! That is what the Egyptians have done to some extent by the embalming of the body. They accompanied this embalming of magical rites of which we know nothing anymore. By them they attracted around the embalmed body magnetic currents sufficient to create a possibility of a precarious life, scarcely physical.

As long as the form remains with its contour and appearance, the Ka, the double, which is no other than the astral body of the occultists and theosophists, has a terrestrial fulcrum to which it remains attached. As long as the body survives, the Ka enjoys in a hardly measurable way, of material goods. For it to have the joy of food, it must have in his grave, food symbols. Similarly, the pleasure of the flesh is given to him by the images of beings that he desired in his lifetime. Every death is surrounded by what was his pleasure or his concern on earth. And despite its lack of visible form, the Ka has wider possibilities than might be supposed. He deals in the afterlife with philosophy and magic. It was found in the tomb of a certain Myrithis, famous magician, a lamp of seven wicks, a convex mirror, a priestess of Isis tambourine, for her to continue his magical operations. There were also various scrolls on which leaned this faceless Ka, to complete his studies*.

This life of the double was a judgment of nature. It delayed the law of transformations, it immobilized the being in the sphere of natural attractions, but sooner or later the being had to leave for the journey to which no one escapes.

Besides the Ka, everyone has a Ba, which is the soul and that the Egyptians symbolized by a bird, sparrowhawk, swallow or ibis, because of its ability to easily jump through space. It is in this soul that the consciousness of man is found and this soul is immortal. It is a ray emanated of Amun-Ra, the hidden spirit, the inner essence of the sun. It is this soul of divine nature which, after the final separation of the body and the double, undertakes the journey of the afterlife.

Whatever the terms of the various symbolisms and the names of the Gods whose unusual soundings only serve to repel us. No matter if instead of the Charon of the Greeks, it is Osiris who leads the Egyptian deaths and that the underground river on which must embark the soul, takes its source, west of Abydos. The important thing to remember is that to achieve the purpose of the journey, a certain amount of spiritual knowledge is essential.

Only this knowledge will allow the dead to tame, by the power of the gaze, the monsters by whom he will be surrounded. Woe to he who does not possess it! Woe to the ignorant! His virtue will not be sufficient for him. He will remain in the realm of shadows and vain terrors.

The one who knows, on the contrary, will respond with wisdom to the questions of the strange driver of a new boat in which he will cross the river that separates the Champs-Elysées. It will finally come before a court presided over by Osiris and composed of forty-two judges. To each judge corresponds a mistake that the man may have committed on

---

* Masters of Egyptology disagree on the interpretation of symbols, the meaning of texts and inscriptions. "The often adventurous guesses cover wrongly the large gaps of the safe science. Fundamental questions remain unanswered." CHANTEPIE DE LA SAUSSAYE, *History of Religions*.

earth and he denies having committed. Each judge is the opposite of a fault, that is to say a quality. The dead confesses and his heart is put on this inexorable balance that is found in all the descriptions of the other world made by all religions. It is by virtue of the lightness of its weight that the soul gets its freedom from terrestrial links. If the gravity of his desires and of the evil forces which are in them do not hold it back, it becomes a luminous Khu, it rises, it soars in the solar region towards the Amun-Ra, it becomes by identification, the sun itself.

If the soul does not have in itself the possibility of this identification, it is condemned by nature to roam in the seventy-five divisions of hell where it undergoes various tortures that all hell symbolisms describe as materials, by a too glaring illogicality to be discussed. Then it is drawn back into the bodies of men or animal bodies.

This return is not based on Egyptian texts absolutely formal. One can say that there are no formal texts on the ancient belief of Egypt. Herodotus and later Servius have claimed that the Egyptians believed in the doctrine of the transmigration of souls. Certain passages of the "Book of Breathing" and even of the "Book of the Dead" confirms it, but it was not enough for many students of the Egyptian religion. I say purposely students as Egyptologists scholars remain uncertain and contradictory before the mystery of the texts. The Book of the Dead which is the basis of any study seems incomprehensible at first.

Perhaps one should accuse the translators. Despite this, many occultists explain it with ease and admiration, and find no darkness in it. "Monument of extravagance and imposture", says Salomon Reinach of this venerable and mysterious book.

Nothing is more disappointing than to see that it is true for all the documents of the ancient wisdom. One has to choose between various interpretations. On one hand, the one of the visionaries, full of faith, who happily wage the marvelous and make spring from it illusory sparks, and on the other hand, the ones of scientists so learned and who watch the scrolls with glasses so exact that they end up seeing nothing.

The Spirit of the Bones in the Kabbalah

The Kabbalah, that is to say the secret doctrine of the Jews, draws its tradition in a primitive revelation: "The Kabbalists say about it: God taught the doctrine first in the angelic world. After the fall of the angels, it was Adam who knew the mysteries. From Adam it passed to Noah, to Abraham and to Moses. From patriarchs to prophets, and, later on, its transmission was effected without interruption*."

One likes to rely on a philosophy which foundations are ancient. But the goal should not be exceeded. The trust one can have in a tradition is reduced if one learns that this tradition has been dictated by God himself.

Apart from the pride of their origin, the Jewish books are marked by a formidable severity which is contradictory to the spirit of kindness that our logic hope to meet more and more as growing in the hierarchies of the intelligent beings. Nature, it is true, is ruthless in the effects of its laws, but if one bows to the inevitable effects of a blind cause, one revolts rightly if one distinguishes violence, the lack of forgiveness, the love to punish, in a higher intelligence than ours and that would devolve the task of governing mankind. "The rigor is essential to the punishment of the guilty", one reads in the Zohar, the book where Rabbi Simeon bar Yohai has gathered, according to the oldest books, the oldest traditions of the Jewish race. And one also sees that the pagans, for being pagans, transmigrate into swine.

But traditions take the qualities and defects of the race that interprets them. A rigorous and violent people translates them in rigor and violence. The expression of eternal truth can be found in Jewish books.

According to Kabbalah, man has apart from his physical body, several invisible bodies interpenetrating between them and which dissociates at the time of death. There is a vital and passionate body (Nephesh), there is the soul (Ruach) and there is the mind, that is to say the true

* PAUL VULLIAUD, *La Kabbale juive.*

being (Neshamah). These three parts of the man are not absolutely distinct, they mingle with each other, like the colors of the solar spectrum, which although successive, merge by gradations. They correspond to three different worlds of which they are the human expression. The subtlest degree of Nephesh corresponds to the lower degree of Ruach and the subtlest level of Ruach corresponds to the least subtle degree of Neshamah. The higher mind, Neshamah, is in contact with the state of absolute spirituality which is divinity. What the Kabbalists call the fall has alienated man from the divine state. He will regain that state when all that was spiritual in him will be pure.

The work of death extends over a much longer period than what is usually thought. Neshamah, the spirit leaves first the body, before the time that is designated with the name of death. The soul, after having spread in every organ, which is the jolt of agony, takes refuge in the heart which is the center of life. Its separation from the body may be sometimes painful, because of the dual appeal of higher spiritual regions and physical lower regions between which it hesitates. At the last minute, the soul leaves the heart through the mouth with the last breath. The Talmud distinguishes 900 different species of death. When death is painful, the dying person experiences the sensation of a thick rope of hair extracted from the throat.

After the departure of the soul, the man seems dead and yet Nephesh is still in him. This vital essence has retained affinities for the body and it will take the work of decomposition and of the Mazzikim, or evil spirits, to get him to leave. But this disintegration is absolute only after a long time. It usually lasts until the complete decomposition. Even then, something Nephesh subsists, which goes down in the tomb, in the bones. This is the imperishable principle of the material body and this forms the Habal of Garmin or body of the resurrection*.

---

* The dogma of the resurrection of the flesh is of an improbability in theory, brilliant. However, it can be understood in the sense of a resurrection by the memory. In times so remotely prodigious, that one cannot evaluate, the human consciousness may have acquired such a development that it will be able it its sole find by the memory its ancient states and this memory will be able to have an ability powerful enough to recreate the past realities in a more real way than

However, the three main bodies of the man, separated by death, have joined the three worlds to which they are attracted to by their particular nature. But before the soul comes and goes during the first seven days after which follow death between the house where the dead lived and the tomb where the body rests. The soul had at the time of death the permission to see his parents and friends who died with the aspect in which it knew them. It also sees the living who are sad and who cry over it in the home of the melancholic return without form.

The spirit of the bones remains attached to the body and it knows in the grave, a dark feeling of rest that should not be disturbed. "That is why it was forbidden to the Jews to bury one from the other people who during their lives had been enemies, or to place a holy man beside a criminal. One took care on the contrary to bury together all those who had loved each other, because in death this attachment continued." One could mention the spirit of the bones, and this was a great disturbance for the death, because, despite the separation of the bodies, Nephesh, Ruach, and Neshamah remained united by a subtle link, to this spirit of the bones. Also the evocation of it was strictly forbidden.

"If this was allowed for us, says the Zohar, we could see at night, when comes the Sabbath, or at the new moon or on feast days, the Diuknims (spectra) stand in the tombs to glorify the Lord."

The vital body, the soul and the spirit having joined their respective world still remain united among themselves and form one. Because the worlds they live in overlap and no distance separates them. Their intimate relations are regulated by the "Tzelem which is their common envelope and which answers to the physical appearance of the original man." The Zohar says of the Tzelem "that its beauty depends on the good works that man has done down here*."

To the extent that man purified himself during life, his mind is allowed to enter the Garden of Eden called palace by the Zohar and which are

---

our terrestrial reality. The spirit of the bones would only be the link between the consciousness to its past.

* C. DE LEININGEN. *Communication addressed to the Munich Psychological Society.*

staged according to the different degrees of spirituality. There are seven palaces of which only six are accessible to man. He crosses the seventh only for a few seconds. If the purification on earth has not been sufficient, the being, after being thrown into one of the seven hells that correspond to the seven Eden, is sentenced to return to earth in a new body.

Although modern Kabbalists do not believe in the doctrine of transmigration, it is frequently a question about this doctrine, in the Zohar.

"The souls here below which transmigrate into the bodies of animals, take the figure of clothing which surrounds them, the figure of pure animals. The spirits of the Pagans which transmigrate here below, take the figures of impure animals." (Zohar, I, 20b).

"The soul of the man without children cannot come back down to earth in a human body. In this case, the soul of the human returns to earth in the form of a mother and the one of the mother returns in the form of a son." (Zohar, III, 100 b).

And it is said a little further that this change of sex is so painful that no other physical pain can be compared to it.

"When the soul has not completed its mission during his time on earth, it is uprooted and transplanted back to earth, as it is written in Job: And the man returns to earth! The transmigrations are inflicted on the soul as punishment and vary according to its guilt. Every soul that has been guilty during his time in this world is, in punishment, forced to transmigrate as many times as necessary in order to achieve, by its perfection, the sixth level of the region from where it emanates." (Zohar II, 94 a).

What must be remembered from that last quote is that life on earth is considered as a punishment, a stay of trials. It will be quite illogically that the Jewish doctrine recommend in all possible shapes, with threats of terrestrial and supraterrestrial punishments, the procreation of children dedicated to these trials.

But the Zohar also teaches, and we will see later the importance of this teaching that, as an exception to the general law, the souls emanating from the seventh spiritual region, and which are by their source of a more refined essence, escape the law of transmigration. This seventh region, which is not limited in space but is a state of being, a source of potential, allows everyone to claim a high source and to justify it by the testimony of its spiritual quality. It opens to all those who are deemed worthy, the door to the highest hope, the hope of escaping the new earthly lives and to achieve a better state, to a higher level in the hierarchy of creatures.

The return to animalism in Pythagoras and in Plato

Ancient Greeks believed that after the cremation of the dead body subsisted a shadow, the Eidolon which survived to the destruction of the body and descended in the Hades. This Eidolon was only an appearance "which reproduced with exactitude the image of the living body, but one supposed formed of a subtle and fine matter similar to those of the swarms*". The dead of Homer are insignificant and juvenile and they get bored among the asphodels of the Champs-Elysées. Only, amongst all those that Ulysses evokes, the divine Tiresias has all his consciousness because he has developed the knowledge of the afterlife. In all the traditions can be found, the assurance that this knowledge of the afterlife is the only way to escape, in the first region of death, to an inevitable period of uncertainty and of fear.

It is only at the beginning of the fifth century before Jesus Christ that Pythagoras came to tell to the Hellenic west, of the immortality of the soul which already professed secretly the Orphic sects and the Dionysiac religion.

Pythagoras, as all the initiators, only specified a scattered notion among the philosophers and towards which aspired men. But the first one, showed a precise path, he gave a method of life to develop ones soul and allow it to conquer its immortality. He indicated a form of salvation appropriate to a race. After so many centuries, it is that form which remains the more accessible to our comprehension and the most easy to practice.

Apart from the Eidolon to which one believed during the Homeric period, man, according to him, owned a spiritual body in which condensed all the energies that were not physical. This spiritual body which was not a temporary individuality, could animate any physical body. Thrown in olden days from the world of Gods, the being was in the body as

* MAURY, *Histoire des religions de la Grèce antique.*

in a prison, in virtue of his past mistakes, or rather his desires. When death separated the psyche of its physical envelop, it spend some time in an invisible region, the Hades, to purify itself. Then it returned to the higher world to be later called to earth and look a new body there. The atmosphere of our world was full of wandering psyches, which fly about among the living, looking for a form where they could satisfy their will to live. It is that desire for life which hastened the incarnations and rushed the psyches to transmigrate in men's bodies or animal's bodies. Furthermore this choice was not available to all. It was determined by the actions of the previous life.

Pythagoras indicated carefully in what manner one had to live, to which moral rules one had to conform in order to reach the path of salvation. The body was a prison in the flesh, the reincarnations being changes of prison, the ideal being to escape to this endless succession of diverse captivities and often fearsome, to reach a free and perfect life in the world of the Gods. The frugality, the abstinence of pleasures and the detachment from material goods, which had to be as much as possible pooled, were at the foundation of these prescriptions. It did not forbid in an absolute way, the pleasure of physical love, but it warned against the loss of spiritual forces of which it is the cause.

As the Buddha, Pythagoras remembered his former lives. He had been Euphorbus, hero of the siege of Troy and according to the legend, he recognized as having belonged to him, the shield of that warrior hung in the temple of Delphi. He had been Hermotimus of Clazomenae which practiced the ecstasy and whose soul had the power to come out of his body.

He did not say if his existence in the body of Pythagoras was his last human existence*.

Empedocles of Agrigento has on the contrary, asserted it with certainty. It was one of the greatest minds of humanity. To transport it in modern times one should imagine someone who would be at the same

---

* A modern legend has confirmed that Pythagoras had been reincarnated in Iamblicus, Neoplatonist philosopher and today, in the Hindu Koot Houmi. This is a legend.

time Pasteur, Jaurès and Ramakrishna. Ardent Pythagorean, he thought as his master in metempsychosis.

This doctrine is considered today as an aberration of the ancient philosophy. Our moral and religious education, the high idea that we make of ourselves make us reject with horror the idea that a human being is reincarnated in an animal.

Yet by thinking, isn't the essence of many individuals only reduced to this? Desires of eating and drinking, sexual attractions, emotional feelings for beings of the opposite sex who meet these attractions, emotional feelings for the children of their flesh, that is to say that they are physically themselves. All this finds its realization in the animal state. Why after death wouldn't they be rushed into an animal germ whose future organization will satisfy all their aspirations? Besides such individuals would be strangely disoriented in a higher world where reality is pure thought. This higher world they would choose if one questioned them, would be for them an incomprehensible hell of which they seek to escape quickly.

Our contemporaries feel great embarrassment mingled with sadness by finding the doctrine of the transmigration of souls in Plato. That this summit of speculation, that fixed star in the sky of pure ideas, that intelligence from which all intelligence is dependent if it is cultivated, could have believed that the soul of man, with its prerogative of reason, transmigrates in an animal body, appears as a betrayal of the spirit, the most serious, if however, it is a game to mock.

The man has developed through the centuries a hubris, perhaps from the time when he thought that the soul was immortal. On behalf of the privilege of thinking, he takes pride of his rank in the hierarchy of beings, without thinking that he hardly uses his privilege and it can be of the thought as of many instruments of precision that become unusable by inaction.

For Plato as for the Pythagoreans, the soul must go through successive rounds of lives, of very diverse nature. "It depends on its own merits, of the successes won by it in its fight against the passions and desires of the body that its terrestrial races lead it up towards the noblest forms of existence. But it can go down to the beast in its incorporations*."

Already in the last Neoplatonists, the possibility of such a lapse appeared an attack on human dignity. Proclus by explaining the Timaeus says that they are only symbolic fictions and others have said it after him . Yet there is neither fiction nor symbol in the following passages of the *Republic* and the *Timaeus*.

"Souls indifferently passed from the bodies of animals in bodies of men and vice versa. Those of the villains in wild species, those of good people in domesticated species, which led to mixtures of any kind."

"God established that the one who would have failed would be changed into a woman in a second birth and if he did not stop being mean, according to the nature of its vices, he would be changed in a new birth in the animal to which it would look like by its manners."

Is there reason to be so surprised by this view? We are still, despite our pride, very close to the animalism.

Egyptians before Darwin honored their ancestors in different animal species. One can find in most Negro tribes of Africa the belief that some men are of the same family as some animals and the one who stemmed him from the breed of crocodiles would commit great evil, by killing a crocodile as by killing its human father. Is the impression of the animal life is not deeply etched on the faces of men? Each of us has among its relationships birds of prey with two feet, miserable bleating sheep, dogs without loyalty. I surprised myself sometimes when a friend offered me his hand, that hand is not webbed and that those who were like donkeys by stupidity, do not have its hooves or ears. In exchange for some reason and an unclear ability to read books, many old birds have lost the ability to fly and sing, many former snakes do not know the bliss of slumber in the backwaters. I met nostalgic lions being powerless though fierce and swans who lost whiteness, and retained only indolence.

Perhaps that Plato has not really understood the human dignity. What transmigrated, according to him, in the bodies of animals was only the lower part of the soul, the terrestrial individuality and it did not trans-

* E. ROHDE, *Psyche: The Cult of Souls and the Belief in Immortality among the Greeks.*

migrate after drinking the waters of Lethe that gives oblivion. Human souls likely to rush into the bodies of animals to satisfy faster sexual desires or family affections did not deprive a spiritual being of divine rank. This spiritual being, they had not created it in them, as was their task. In some cases, they had deleted its essence. The community of souls with human bodies was their touchstone and their means to differentiate.

Once the differentiation performed, each went, according to its spare effort and the momentum of its aspirations, towards its true fate, one above and the other below. The philosophy and the practice of wisdom striped the man of what is corruptible and mortal and only them could place him, out of space and time, in the divine state.

The spherical body of Origen

Once came a time when death took the character of a passage towards the eternal damnation. One could have even been predestined to this damnation, carrying around the invisible seal of the punishment. It was quite obvious for the intelligent that the chosen ones were very few who would sit at the right of the Christian God and one had to consider the hypothesis when one would enter forever in the theological hell. Hell was for a long time known to all. But there were rivers, palm trees, terrible landscapes, it is true, but suffused with a spectacular poetry. Carrying a rock and dropping it from a mountain top, pouring water in a pierced barrel, were tasks of slaves, but tasks still human. The Danaids, their vase on the shoulder, could undoubtedly joke among each other and make fun in a low voice of Persephone. They had extinguished coals for makeup and the ashes carefully crushed were an ancient recipe to make more delicate the facial skin.

The new hell was absolutely terrifying by the monotony, the regularity, the eternity of the pain, even if one imagined that the fire was symbolic of the moral solitude, that thirst was desire, that demons with their horns and their tridents were your equals in evil. Christianity made triumph a haunting notion of hell.

Origen was sentenced by councils for disagreeing on this dogma with the members of the Church who had just build it by kicking it with an Episcopal stick. His hell was not eternal enough and in a future minute of the longevity of times, Satan himself would come out of it to enter the bosom of God. Origen was a mystic ascetic who only saw on earth the sin and the redemption of the sin by punishments. During his lifetime, to punish himself for the sexual desire he imposed to his body the torture of castration. He undoubtedly thought that everyone endured it in hell. He thought that the souls had preexisted and having the gratification of the divine love, they fall because of enjoyment in the incarnation, that is to say in evil. The man was punished during his life, and he was even more after death. The fire of desire consumed him and this fire had to extinguish, for lack of food. This lasted for a long time and this period was necessary, because a punishment too short damaged as much as a too rapid recovery for a patient. He had imagined that at the moment of the resurrection, those who were destined to fire would resurrect "with immortal bodies that the tortures would not succeed to destroy."

But perhaps he expressed himself in this way for the vulgar souls, because Origen admitted two categories of believers, the ones who were likely of high speculations and the crow of the others. Originally Platonist, he did not hide his preference for the first ones and his contempt of ignorance. One arrived to God after death, in virtue of its moral perfection and of its culture. The bodies in the afterlife varied according to the qualities of everyone. The man who had accomplished in his life the necessary purifications had an ethereal body, of a spherical form, spherical as the human skull which was its physical symbol and as the planets of heavens. This body looked like the one of which have spoke Saint Paul, the body of the spirit. It was "the luminous body" of Pythagoras and "the light chariot of the soul" of Plato. It was this body which, by condensing its subtle sphere, took a new place in the flesh.

Elsewhere can be found the idea of this spherical body. Plutarch* speaks of a man in catalepsy who, when he came to, told that he saw the souls of the dead as luminous balls. These balls while shattering, allowed a human form to escape, of vaporous essence. Tertullian reports the similar vision of a sleepwalker. Nowadays, many magnetized subjects, when they are questioned on the state in which they find themselves, answer that they are a luminous ball in the middle of the shadows†.

Origen, as the first fathers of the Church‡, Clement of Alexandria,

---

* PLUTARCH, *On the Delay of the Deity in the Punishment of the Wicked.*

† Experiments of doctor Baraduc.

‡ Saint Jerome says that "the doctrine of transmigration was secretly taught in small numbers since the most ancient times as a traditional truth and he recommends not to reveal it."

Saint Justin Martyr says that when the soul is too far from God it transmigrates

Gregory of Nazianzus, Justin Martyr, believed in the transmigration of the human soul through different bodies. He did not think that there was a specific immutability which prevented it to change its human destination. It went up, it could come down and come back to animal bodies.

The soul, part of the divine, prepared its return in the human form. There it created a spiritual sphere, more or less ethereal. This sphere, at the time of death, made a stay in hell where it lightened with its own substance the flame which had to consume it. This flame was the remorse of bad accomplished actions and it burned for a long time and of a cruel fire. This was an inner fire, without glare. It did not light up the "external darkness" which were the darkness of ignorance. The sphere was purified by consuming itself, but a distant time will come when the spheres which became more and more pure would lose all body appearance, would have no material reality. They would become pure spirit. Then they would reach a perfect state, the one of the found Christ where the corporeality has no sense anymore and which is the formless state of Brahmanists.

But the Church representatives, meeting at the Council of Constantinople in 553, under the presidency of Justinian could not bear the thought that after endless ages, those they called the wicked, spiritualized in turn, would be forgiven and would return to the bosom of God. The ancient Hebraic revenge had to brave the time and survive to the last judgment. They put to the index the doctrines of Origen and also the one of reincarnation. The spherical body of the sinner was doomed to become more and more dark, more and more opaque. Devoured by a flameless glow, it had to rotate endlessly around a sun of condensed darkness, among stone planets, in a materialized vacuum, in a hopeless void.

***

in bodies of beasts.

"The spiritual beings, says Origen, wanted to materialize. The worst ones became demons. The others were men who, through repeated incarnations into human bodies became angels again. They are forced to move from sphere to sphere and take varying envelopes, according to the worlds they inhabit."

Thus, as far back in the time of ancient philosophies and religions, one can find about death, if not, a very similar design, at least one identity on the most essential points. The venerable age of beliefs does not constitute an absolute proof. Everyone might have been wrong. But the most skeptical must be impressed by the consistency of the statements and the value of those who have claimed it.

Among the Hindus, the Egyptians, the Chaldees, the Greeks, in the Kabbalah, in the religion of the Druids, the first Christians, in Plato, in Plotinus and his disciples, in all the sects which joined secretly their hands through all the Middle Ages, the same enrolment is found to the following ideas, known by different names and expressed in various ways.

The man has several invisible bodies which, at the time of death, separate from the physical body. These invisible bodies that constitute the soul, stay in successive worlds. These worlds are for ones situated in a remote point in space, for others, they interpenetrate each other. The knowledge of things of the afterlife is the only quality which allows no to suffer. The ultimate aim is the return to the divine unity and this return is undertaken through successive lives, either on earth or in other worlds, either in a human form or other forms.

All the religions and all the great sages of Antiquity were unanimous to consider the earth as a miserable stay of sufferings to which one should escape. Life is not the reality and one sees the world backwards. Death is desirable. Therefore, there is a fundamental opposition between the belief of the religions and the wise and the one of the majority of men which yet observe the rites of the religions and honor the wisdom of the wise. For this majority, life is not the means, but the purpose. Death is impressive. This contradiction should be highlighted in order to know on which side one should line up, with the crowd of ignorant or with the intelligent and the perfect ones.

The true secret of death

I will resume the true secret of death as it has circulated among men since the beginning of the world. This secret is extraordinary because of the mysterious faculty it possesses. In virtue of this faculty that is all its own, it may be announced with clarity, it is never kept in the human memory and the one to whom it is exposed and who understood it remains exactly at the same point of ignorance, as if there had been neither pronouncement nor understanding. However, its word is more truthful than an innocent heart, more fix than the axis of the earth, more revealing of stellar depths than any astronomer telescope. It has inhabited the mind of many philosophers, members of many sects have known it and have bequeathed it to one another as a legacy, wise of all times have passed it to each other from hand to hand. But can the fluid water be passed from hand to hand? Men continue to consider death as a fearsome enigma, because of the astonishing priority the secret has to fade as soon as it has been pronounced.

When the man is about to die of what is called natural death, even though all deaths are natural, he usually has a lying position. He should rather be on his knees to thank, because of this cruel mother nature which so far has shown so stingy of it, he receives a precious benefit.

At the time when he leaves the beings and thing he loved, he feels inside of him a mysterious decrease of the attraction to live. It had never happened during his life. When he lost his fortune, henceforth the possession of money had not seemed useless to him. When his beloved mistress had left him, he had not desired with less force. On the contrary, the desire became more intense because it was no longer feasible. For the first time, a happy harmony occurs. At the time when the indifference can preserve him from despair, something similar slips in him. He has neither the time to be surprised, nor to rejoice, not even to be aware of it. The dissociation of his true being and his physical body occurs with the same neutral simplicity as the phenomenon of birth by the union of seeds, in the dark cradle of the matrix.

As in the curious phenomenon of dormancy, to which we are used to but which is extraordinary, the organ of sight first ceases to function. The organ of hearing is the last to persist and the man who dies and who has all the appearances of death, still hears the pronounced words around him, but veiled and as if they were pronounced through cotton.

In the form of a light fog tinted in purple and almost always invisible, he leaves his body by the top of the forehead and leaves it at a right-angled corner. The attraction of the earth is no longer felt as the same strength and he rises. Sometimes, particularly sensitive witnesses have seen the mysterious departure, at the last second of the agony. Charles Henry, during his experiments could assign a weight to the invisible form which has just entered the other world.

"May he rest in peace and may the light of God's glory shine over his forehead", says the admirable Christian prayer. The one who survives to a being he has loved and looks how he can help him does not need to make another wish. During the dreadful life, the man fell asleep each night. The shock dissociating death gives him a similar sleep. He is sleeping. He does not know. He does not see. He will not see anymore, as he has lost the material organs through which the living perceives and communicate with each other. Those who continue to live close to the death is surprised and becomes desperate since the soul survives, it cannot exceptionally in their favor, produce some manifestation testifying its existence in the afterlife.

There is between one world and another a separation all the more inexorable that the space is not to blame and that these worlds inter-penetrating, exist in the same place. The one who left cannot return. He must not return. If he tried to do so, it is that he would still be wandering in the terrestrial currents, beset by premature temptations of incarnation. Instead of regaling himself by his mortuary presence, the living should beg him by prayer not to try this vain return and to let go in the river of the world.

The one who just died does not sleep forever. He has lost his physical form and his dormancy takes place on a plan where the relations between the man, the time and the space are different. Thus, it is possible to formulate the rule which reign over them: As one rises in a subtler state of matter, time is faster, the space is less measurable and more easily crossed. The state of ideal perfection must be cleared of any notion of time and space.

Man's dormancy after death has therefore a relative duration for each. In the same way as in life, the one who has an exciting occupation for his morning, wakes up earlier than the one who has nothing to do, likewise after death, the one who has tasks or duties, wakes up to fill them. This awakening is mixed with astonishment and terror as to whether it was with dread that the soul looked at death in his lifetime.

The man is in a new world, governed by a different principle than the one on earth. The concentration, the effort of all that was alive in order to materialize was the law of the physical life. Abruptly, he must obey to a reverse movement of order, the one of the centrifugal force and of the expansion.

He is in the middle of darkness and he perceives, not with his senses, but with an inner faculty still embryonic, the movement of the universal life which develops around him with a rapidity of vibrations unknown so far. He feels passages of creatures whose forms are new to him. Currents drag him away. Attractions and repulsions are sovereign and he is launched one to another. A vast night is around him and he madly tries to go towards it. It is only by effort of his inner thought he manages to change the shadows which surrounds him in an unclear twilight. It is according to his degree of knowledge that he is the victim of unknown terrors or that he participates immediately the joyous and light drunkenness of a new life.

Woe to he who has never thought of death and who did not prepare for it by a terrestrial wisdom. All religions and all philosophies have been unanimous throughout the ages. Only the knowledge of what is to come, the reflected intelligence, allows to pass without pain, guided by the light one project oneself, the kingdom where one has not more eyes to see.

When the soul comes out slowly from the incoherence of slumber, it is crossed by the ray of remembrance. This is the essential minute, the decisive point of the future life. This awakening still keeps an analogy with the awakening of the living man after an ordinary night. The living man, who comes out of the slumber, recreates his personality by the memory of his concerns of the day, the representations of actions he is going to accomplish during the day. The dead man needs a vaster representation and it is the proceedings of his entire existence he sees as a succession of frames more or less rapid in front of his eyes. And it is this proceeding which constitutes the judgment of death.

But for this judgment, Gods of any religion are present. The forty-two Egyptian judges do not sit in the mystical valley around Osiris, dominated by the effigies of the crocodile and the snake. Minos, Aeacus and Rhadamanthus are not present, and the symbolic scales of sins does not oscillate its pans on its eternal axis. The lonely man contemplates his life, the following of his actions, the following of his thoughts, and what contribution each and others have brought to the perfection of his soul. He judges himself to the extent that he has a faculty of judgment. The balance is in him, he divides himself the good and evil; he loads the pans and he holds the needle.

The one who does not recognize a fault, has not committed them. No punishment is reserved in the afterlife for the greatest criminals, if his conscience is clear.

Ignorance is the only mistake of which the good and bad ones are also punishment by distraction, shadow and fear. Because nature, with the slowness of its reactions, oppose to our hope of justice a visible but inexorable justice. What we call, in our infantile language, the punishment of wicked, only happens in the afterlife with the birth of consciousness, that is to say after many lives. The one who is punished has only personal pain in the form of remorse and as the remorse is created only by consciousness, he is only punished, all in all, when he starts being good.

In the transitional world where the man finds himself after death, there is a specific suffering of the place which is practiced also on the virtuous ones and on perverts. It is the one which comes from the nonfulfillment of desires. Any desire which needs a physical body in order to be satisfied causes to the man deprived of a body, a longing which is similar to the caress of the flame or the one of the vital ice. This is what was called *the torment of hell*. But this suffering cannot be of long duration. The more the desire has material causes and the more it exhausts itself rapidly.

The man who has not cultivated in his life neither his intelligence nor his affections is dragged away by the attractions of the terrestrial life. He only aspires to satisfy himself by the pleasure to live in the flesh and he rushes himself blindly on a living seed by the development by which he will regain existence. The attraction law by which the fellowmen are attracted to one another is such that the violent will be called by a seed in which his violence will be reached, that the lustful will fall of himself in the seed conformed by lust. Incidentally, no other possibility opens for those ones.

But the man who arrives in the afterlife with the richness of his affections is located in the country where affection is a reality. The body he owns, body of magnetic nature, could be called emotional body. It is the Linga Sharira of the Hindus, the Nephesh of the kabbalists, the astral body of theosophists. The attraction and the repulsion are essential laws of this new world. If the deceased have kept affections for beings left on earth, they will naturally be taken to these beings, they will live in their atmosphere, they will know this gentleness they called in their lifetime "the pleasure of being together". This pleasure of being together is linked to their general capacity to love. If they have developed in themselves the love of their fellowmen they will attract to them other wandering creatures, they will join groups whose mutual sympathy will be a source of well-being. This will extend during a variable time according to the affective power of each and according to the possibilities of his intelligence.

Because what matters is to rise out of this intermediate region, to change the twilight of dead light that bathes the dead in the living light of the spiritual region. As each fire burns of its own fire of which it is the food, everyone sees with clarity what one has in oneself and one lights oneself.

The form in which the man remains after death takes the contour of the human body. The ordinary man enjoys in it neither full consciousness nor will. He is in a state which is both the waking and the dream state. But what must be remembered is that everything which is indicated varies with each individual. There are as many different destinies for the dead as for the living.

The one who has cultivated the mind, who has created in his lifetime a spiritual entity capable of exceeding the circles of astral currents, will feel that entity awaken and the consciousness will reappear. This awareness will never be the same, it will be subtler and clear of earthly cares. Also, as it will live again, the body will change, will lose its human character, will become ovoid, more spherical as the body described by Origen. It is in this aspect that it will reach the luminous world of thought, having undergone the second death, the death of his emotional body.

"They are really happy the men who have crossed the golden bridge and have reached the seven golden mountains of that place separated from us by at least thousands of myriads of solar systems. There flourishes the divine flower of Udumbara which plunges a root in the shadow of the earth." Thus expressed himself the Buddha.

This is the Devachan, the paradise of the Christians, the plastic stay of Platonic ideas, where thought has more reality than the matter on our earth. The seven golden mountains of the Buddha are the symbol of seven different states, that is to say seven modes of vibration more and more subtle. The principle of this transcendent world is more about beauty than bliss. Happiness comes there especially from the participation in the cosmic life and a living sense of brotherhood. Such happiness is accessible to few men. The entrance of this ideal world is never the reward of virtue. The vast and sometimes incomprehensible law that moves the universes is absolutely foreign to our sense of right and wrong. It is an indifferent law of cause and effect. The only good ones are those who comply to this law. The only bad ones are those who turn themselves away from it. It is true that there is often a coincidence between what men call virtue and the state of comprehension and love which opens the door of the Devachan. But how many of them have led a perfect life on earth and who during this perfection too human haven't modeled in themselves the subtle essence, the divine body which would allow them to enjoy of the spirit. Those are not rejected on an inexorable threshold… This threshold does not exist for them. They do not have the possibility to see it and if they do, its aspect would be without attraction. In virtue of their terrestrial affinities, they are brought back by the desire of materialization, they come back down towards the physical manifestation, eager to incarnate in physical forms.

The others, the owners of the spherical body, blossom, expand, become enthused by blossoming, the dilatation and the elation of these flowers of Udumbara, of which spoke the Buddha in this imagery which makes it so often incomprehensible for us. They live among protean imaginations, the ideal creations composed of prisms which have forty-nine colors, cadenced by music resonating of forty-nine notes. The intensity of the vibrations of life is so great that the happiness of man combined to it has a vertiginous character. The essence of this happiness is hard to describe because nothing in the physical world is close to it. Those who tried to describe it fell in rough errors as the one of Dante who places in his paradise sovereigns, because they have been good sovereigns, militant monks, because they fought well for their religion and in the middle of the angel's round, they discuss points of scholasticism.

What can be said about the happiness of spiritual worlds in which it is given to man to reach, at the last stage of his human race, a spiritualized form, but still existing, here is that this happiness is produced by the intimate alchemy of intelligence and of love reached to their highest degree.

But all happiness which possibility has been generated on earth eventually consumes itself through the times and attains its extinction. Plato set to thousand years the length of one life to another for a common man. Modern theosophists indicate the approximate number of fifteen hundred years*. After a period, difficult to evaluate and variable for

---

* According to the clairvoyant philosopher Steiner, Voltaire seems to have lived at the time of the invasion of Arabs in Spain. He would have reincarnated him-

each, the Buddhist flower of Udumbara remembers that it has a root which holds it to the earth and which gives it a sap of life. The human soul has exhausted its spiritual power. It is now only a virtual repository, a possibility of existence. This enigmatic ardor to live and to develop which is the world's principle and it carries with it to its central point, will project it again in a terrestrial incarnation.

Shankaracharya, one of the greatest philosophers of India has announced with melancholy:

— It is difficult for sensitive creatures to attain a human birth.

Thus he admitted that the human soul only entered with difficulty in a body, whether because there are more souls than bodies or because of an own difficulty to this union, which is, in itself, the strangest that one can imagine. It is at the time of this thrust in the incarnation that must act the law in which one wanted to see a reward or a punishment. Does everyone have the life he deserved by the actions and thoughts of his previous life? There is no merit and no demerit. There are causes and effects. According to one's fury of living and the call of one's attractions, each soul rushes itself in the seed where it will be able to set up and it conforms to its nature by possession. The haste, the imperious desire to materialize are causes of falls in lower seeds.

But it is before this fall that the key problem arose not only of our life, but of the chain of all our lives. In what measure can we escape the return on earth, avoid innumerable evils of incarnation and attain a life of a higher order? This is the true purpose of man and this aim is achievable.

---

self another time, during the middle ages, in a woman's body before Voltaire. This would make a separation of about five hundred years between lives. According to Steiner again, Éliphas Levi would have lived in America just before its discovery by Christopher Columbus and has had two lives before reappearing in the nineteenth century. Spiritualists, according to the indications of mediums, set for the succession of lives, much earlier dates. This information of wonderful order is given, of course, without further proof than the good faith of the ones who gives them. The differences between the lives must be very variable, from five minutes to several centuries and relative to the degree of conscience of every one.

***

Such is the secret of death which was transmitted since the most remote times, the secret that all the religions and all the wise of the earth
have known. Those who learn it, nod their heads and continue to doubt
by saying that they know nothing. This may be due to a native human
stupidity. It is possible that this inability to believe the duration of the
soul and the succession of its lives, is a primary need of the order of
things, as the imponderability of fire or the balance of planets.

Perhaps the certainty of a better existence after death would incite the
entire humanity to commit a rapid suicide. Perhaps a legitimate sense
of responsibility would prevent men to procreate to avoid the fear of
incarnation to those who have not yet fallen. The physical earth would
be deserted. The ends that nature pursuits would be diverted from
their courses. It could no more impose a stay in the bosom of a tortu-
ous matter. Souls by their own divine force would find another way to
grow in perfection. We will see later on, how we can consider this fight
and in what measure the man who modifies the lower laws of nature,
could also change its vital law and make the world he lives in silent and
empty as a sepulcher.

The struggle against life by the suppression of the seed

"Oh my God, since life is so bad, I do not want to give birth to a child who will suffer as I have suffered and, in procreating in turn, will suffer from other creatures."

I heard this word and it broke my heart. It was said, one evening, in a deserted avenue where rain made large and gleaming puddles and where, by a curious mirage, it was the mud which illuminated.

The woman who pronounced these words was sitting next to me on a terrace of a café. She whispered them softly, with a sort of fear and she immediately bowed her head looking aside, as if she feared an immediate punishment for this revolt against the essential law of life. Her voice was husky the color of her skin was dull, and even though she was petite, wretched, for me she seemed to shine of all the beauty of courage.

She did not say more to me, but I understood her determination, the significance of the struggle she undertook. She had measured the creation of the painful being of which her body was going to be the repository. She refused to create this evil that life was, to prepare the tragedy of the future death. She removed the cause which was birth. And I could not help myself but to admire her for having made the sacrifice of maternal joy and only hoping for a victory forever hopeless.

I glimpsed above her head all the powers she was going to brave in order to have in heart more pity than the divine law. It was a curse as old as the world which stroke the one which refused to create. Judges with marble faces were standing in the court with their ready sentence. She would be locked in a cellar and tortured through questionings. And above these judges, there was in the invisibility, another court imagined by the religions, more inexorably slow and more devoid of pity. This one would create diseases with endless repercussions that would undermine the foundations of her body. She would be tortured by remorse and under the name of purgatory or law of the Karma, and they would even abduct her from the posthumous rest. Because in the eyes of the society as in the eyes of God, there is no worse unforgivable crime than the one exercised against the safety of her life.

No human word resonated more deeply in me. I remember that I looked with attention the leaned skull of the woman which had pronounced it and the light of her look to know if she realized the impact of her resolution. The features of her face were ordinary. Blonde highlights fell on the right and the left of the narrow forehead. The thin nose and pouting lips could conceal a lost attraction of pleasure. The sincerity of her voice and all I knew about her gave me the assurance that she had no other motive than pity. Nothing on her, revealed the inner courage, if a drop of rain, between the two eyes, had not sparkled as a star.

Oh my God! She had said. And sometimes her face turned towards the impersonal figures formed by the buildings that were in front of us. I felt that she identified them unconsciously with the God she had just invoked. It was an anonymous organization, an instructing machine of causes, of which one could not expect neither help nor consolation. Behinds these metal doors, under the shelter of these stone facades, were hiding generative couplings, the perpetuation of a mathematical life, of which one could not stop the development.

And that night, the raindrops fell tirelessly from the sky. Thus, I thought, the seeds of men in human matrices. And this had no end. The inexorable sexual law rushed the creatures in the painful incarnation. Yet, the chain could be interrupted, if the link was rebel and broke of itself thanks to an inner strength of rupture. The wise who in all ages have preached the detachment and the suppression of the desire, had no other purpose but to stop the incarnation.

One objects that man must suffer in order to improve. In virtue of the original sin or its primitive desire to live and to enjoy the life, he is himself the cause of his miseries. The sufferings he endures have not been wanted by the divinity; they are the result of ignorance and egoism of man in his various existences.

But it is the principle of life on the planet that has something inevitably fierce in its essence. This ferocity that increases with the degree of materialization would have brought even without original sin and without human blindness. Hardly a small tree he begins to deploy its branches that the nature that gave it hypocritically sap to push, try to pull it from the ground with the wind, tortures it with cold, burn it with drought. The weakest animal species have beside them better armed animals that eat them. The first light of human intelligence used to fight against the furious anger or the inexplicable vagaries of nature. What is called progress is merely a series of small victories against the natural laws. One fight constantly against these laws but one respect one of them, the one by which perpetuates the life and pain.

It seems that nature intended that it would be attacked in its generating source. If one gives it a cosmic consciousness similar to that of humans, what can be distinguished in this consciousness is the fear of not living, a terror whose manifestations are senseless. Only precautions not to let alter one of the branches of the multifaceted organism of the world! Millions of pollen are thrown to the wind for the reproduction of certain plants and these millions of pollen are not considered sufficient, since besides their number, besides the insured chances they have to be placed in the right places of the fertile land, nature has yet blown insects instinct to propagate them by shaking their wings. The animal species give birth to inordinate posterity. There are outbreaks of locust, rats, fish. And despite this abundance of life, the fear of dying which pulsates the cosmic consciousness remains legitimate since some animal species are suddenly suffering from languor and sexual poverty, since some plant families, after extraordinary expansions, let themselves die mysteriously.

There is an occult force of destruction that shakes God's mind. He is afraid of dying, as well as the man made in his image. Something deadly surrounds him. He creates an illusion of a triumphant life, he brings out the sexes, he pours floods of seeds, but he has not the certainty of being eternal.

The human being is the most complicated creation, the most learned of his visible creation. In order to make him appear with its delicate organs, his matured intelligence by the experiences of successive lives, he has accomplished an immense work. He has endowed of speed the primitive atom. Around a core, like around a sun, it he made rotate his electrons, animated from the power of attracting and repulsing each other. The atoms have formed cells. The cells separated by segmentation. In these multiplied cells and which swim with delight in the protoplasm of the male gland, began to live a little snake, a strange being with an ovoid head, slightly flattened and a mobile appendage through which he leaps. It is this small snake that the divine spirit instructed the mission to perpetuate the human being, the supreme flower of living beings. In bringing the body in the passionate activity and then in the blind weariness of desire, the snake carrying under his flattened face the mystery of human possibilities, must jump into the darkness of the female sex and rejoin there the egg to which it is promised. For one of these messengers reach the goal, the divine spirit, in his terror of not succeeding, has created countless small snakes. The microscope can see a hundred thousand of it per cubic millimeter. And by exception, they are fraternal and do not eat each other. All were looking up at the sky of life. And there is one swifter, more courageous, more enduring which, through the warm moisture of love, crosses the open body of the woman. The generative arrow is so fast, that it to ascend to her heart.

And so begins an incredible work, the transformation of the tiny snake in a human being, with bones and carrying a skull, repository of intelligence. In the crossed epithelial cells, an egg begins to live. The egg becomes an embryo with the characteristics of the snake, then those of a fish, until stumps mysteriously appear, the collar bone of the lower jaw and a slit in the shape of a cleft-lip that will be a mouth to speak and kiss.

But there are only exchanges in blood, so that the embryo becomes a fetus and a strange genital tubercle becomes for no apparent reason in the male or female sex organ! The effort of the mother carrying the fetus that will keep its nine months' burden is not enough. All terrestrial influences are working so that the conceived being comes to term. The blasts of climates, the electric waves, the subtle food of air collaborate to create an organized machine where a consciousness must live. And it is not just the planet that gathers its strengths to this flawed master-piece that will be the man, the other planets in the sky also send their influences by dictating the destiny of the creature, it is the moon that acts on marine periods, it is the sun, protector of children born before noon, it is the whole cosmic immensity.

Nature is afraid of dying and it wants to keep us locked up in the circles of its manifestations. Glory to the creature which, heedless of ancestral prejudices, braves the pain caused by the tearing of the seed, the calling of its maternal instinct and all social and divine punishment! Glory to the one who faithfully takes on the fight against the God of living forms, the dark brother of the spiritual God! Glory to the one who has enough love to deny her beloved and unknown child the ter-restrial torment, and with the exciting and hot seed of blood, to reject him in the kingdom of immaterial light!

This creature stood up suddenly and she gave me her hand, as if I had been at a great distance, on the other side of an abyss. I looked at her moving away on sidewalk of the avenue. She seemed not to be aware of the hostile powers arrayed against her. Did she glimpsed the hand of the midwife, the mixture of poisons which rushed the blood, the ap-pearance of a blind tadpole on a soiled cloth? She went slowly, in the light splashing of drops, carrying in his heart, like a hidden sun, her pity, stronger than life.

Afar, a shop window of a pharmacist made on the sidewalk, with its colored jars, a sort of missed rainbow. As Noah's rainbow, after the flood, it was not the sign of reconciliation, but that of the eternal struggle of nature and man.

The incineration and putrefaction of the body

The horror that the idea of incineration aspire to many people comes from an unconfessed hope of physical eternity and of resurrection of the flesh, in the same beloved flesh that the one we possess at the time when the problem is considered. The simple thought should conceive that the destruction by putrefaction of the body, in a small underground dwelling of wood or stone, is also radical, although slower.

And if a similar seed to this spirit of the bones of which the Kabbalah speaks, was supposed to conserve the model of the being, the essence of its life and of its form, it would be an invisible seed that could resist to any material destruction, to that of fire as the one of the tombstone.

The choice between the different ways of which the body must be removed has a certain importance. The choice should be relative to the development of each and to its detachment of earthly things. The one who dies with a legitimate love for his close relations, for the objects that surrounds him, the living matter which envelops him by surroundings of beauty, will be, if he is burned, suddenly striped of the point of reference he preserved on earth, by the game of affinities. Death separates him forever from all his loves enrolled in the form. But he can still wander in the places where he has lived, float in the atmosphere of those his love, found there the vital joy of their affection.

This research has a desperate attraction. But it is not conscious. For the average being, it takes place until the moment when, attracted by what he desires, he rushes into the new incarnation.

If, on the contrary, the man, by the consumption of the fire, looses all connection with earth, if his corpse becomes dust without any sort of affinity, he is detached from the world of forms. The attractions cease to exercise on him. He will struggle and maybe a formal impossibility to regain the atmosphere of those he has left. There is a risk that he will be taken by the fluidic torrents, out of the circles of his planet. In order to face such a state, he needs to be pure of desires, stripped of affections, illuminated by the serenity of his consciousness.

Then he will perhaps have more difficulties to reincarnate among these forms which he would have wanted to destroy as easily as possible, the last one occupied by him. Because our will survives in ourselves as an active force. His difficulty to reincarnate will come of himself, because he has created a force to destroy forms. This difficulty will naturally not be absolute and will only act as delay, the desire of life always coping, as long as he has not been consciously turned off. But the absence of a common thread will perhaps make him reincarnate in a foreign environment.

I noticed that in France, the few people who cared about being incinerated and notified this desire in their last will were those who, even if they were ignorant, had a vague instinct that incineration was a more complete separation with an earth where they did not taste happiness. They confusedly thought to avoid in a certain measure a too fast return, by the will to destroy the form in their possession.

But incineration which is wise for the sages cannot be practiced in a country where reigns the ignorance of the things of death. The Greeks had set a period of ten days between death and incineration. Among the most barbaric peoples where incineration is used, the dead are kept at least five days before being burned. The rapid incineration, as it is practiced in my neck of the woods, is an act of anticipated imprudence.

May they rest in peace! Say all the prayers of the dead. This rest is necessary for the detachment of the invisible body. The invisible body detach generally immediately. But in those who have a violent desire for life or whose death is sudden, the link is broken with more slowness. There must be a begin of decomposition so that the sensitive body leaves the body of which it was the double for years. It happens that the double is not yet detached after three days, or even more. The incineration can thus be considered as an imprudence, as long as it is practiced by barbaric men who know nothing of the future life and who want to learn nothing from it.

In Malabar and on the Coromandel coast there has been for centuries a practice that has raised a huge disapproval in the world but which hid a deep wisdom. The wife or wives of the dead were burned with him. This practice was only cruel by its exaggeration and by the number of consumed wives. If fifty women were burned following the death of a king, it was difficult to assume that this king was passionately loved by these fifty women, loved even in death. But if a woman or even many women have given themselves for a man, the only assured way not to leave him by death is to die with him and die in the fire community.

Fire has a unity power along with destruction. It is in the intense solar heat that vibrate the supra-divine beings who have attained the highest degree of union. The fire makes the separation of the double and the body, final. But the doubles that cherish themselves are united in this destruction. The creatures which loved each other and have made the dream to stay together, are launched, combined, in sub-terrestrial worlds. They undertake the unity they have designed during their lifetime. They escape to research and change. They know, for a few minutes of physical pain, a long duration of divine happiness. Blessed the lovers whose bodies are devoured along with fire!

Looking back at my life, I see that I have never known any creature devoid enough of the desire to live and rich enough of love and certainty, to climb with me on the stake, as those that stood on the shores of Coromandel. I regret it and there is no selfishness in this regret. I would have been ready to make a reciprocal agreement with the one who, alive, would have faced the fire to follow me. I sincerely believe that an atrocious pain, but temporary, would not be too costly for the union by the flame. We will see furthermore, how, in this union beyond death, hides the ideal secret of nature and how we better attain it.

The Endura of the Albigensians

The best way to defeat death would be to remove its first cause which is birth. The wise, who, of all times have preached the detachment and the suppression of the desire have not had another purpose. If there is no more desire, there is no more generation. They did not get to the bottom of their though fearing to rise the reprobation of all lover's of life.

Those who think that life is poor can put an end to this evil by destroying their own lives by violence. It seems simple in theory. But apart from the necessary courage to practice suicide, it seems that, if one examines with care the problem, it is infinitely more complex than it appears.

By the way, all simplicity too dazzling in a law of nature always hides for the man few dangerous traps.

The idea of suicide seems horrible, especially for those who love life. It scares those who extremely suffer because they are not ensured of finding after death a worse state and in many cases, this is what could happen to them. Those who have the certainty that the states that follows death are better than those of life, could favorably consider suicide. But most of the time they do not do it; and they are right in many cases. But not all.

There is no metaphysical reason to consider suicide as a bad action in itself. It is most of the time a bad action, but it is for useful reasons, because of its upsetting consequences in the afterlife. If one recognizes to the man the right to give himself life by his desire, one cannot discuss him the right to commit suicide, life being strictly the equal of death. If one objects against suicide that there is a divine order of things that should not be interrupted by the human will, it is reasonable to reply that suicide will be considered as a part of this divine order. A man is often driven to suicide by a long series of causes and effects with which he had nothing to do. His act, determined by rigorous events, takes a providential character, that is to say, led by the views of the so-called providence. The divine order has provided in its organization violent deaths, wars, epidemics and suicides along with other fatalities.

Suicide in ancient times did not inspire horror with which it is viewed today, Plato recognized many cases in which it was permitted. "A painful position" or "the fear of an unhappy future" were sufficient reasons for him. The Stoics enumerated five cases where suicide was legitimate and in these five cases appeared poverty.

The philosopher Zeno found for him an additional case, the answer to a kind of appeal heard by him alone. He was seventy years old, the age when usually grows the desire to live, and he lived in Athens a quiet and peaceful existence. Leaving his school, he fell and stayed, within seconds, lying on the ground. One saw him listening and he said: There is no need to call me, I am coming! And with his hand, he gave a few small strokes on the ground to confirm this arrival. He went home and hanged himself.

Among the Gauls, when someone was determined to suicide, he requested the convening of a kind of Areopagus composed of the most sensible people in the city. He explained why he had to leave life and whether those reasons were recognized as valid, he received an official permission. One knows that life after death was considered by the Gauls as a certainty so great, that many transactions were made by a credit which only had its realization in the afterlife.

It is the Jewish people which all Western are moral heirs, which gave to life the enormous price we give it. This price is based on love for the physical pleasure and the secret materialism hidden in the heart of Christians, even the most faithful. Moses' law deprived burial those who committed suicide. The Roman church invented punishments to punish them. During the middle ages, one torn the stones of the threshold of the house of the man who had committed suicide because his body had to be dragged to the gallows and that this body was not worthy to touch the stones God.

Despite these strict laws, it was in the thirteenth century, in the south of France, that spread a sect whose teachings approached most of the wisdom required of man on earth. The believers of this sect are known as the Albigensians*.

The Albigensians of the Languedoc recognized as the Buddhists of India, that the mind and matter are the opposite poles of the same force and they identified good with the spirit and evil with the matter. The man, composed of these two elements was launched by the transmigration into the world of changing forms.

He was held in the perpetual swirl of transformations by his attachment to the principle of existence. To escape the pain of the matter and attain the joy of the spirit, the joy of the divine state, it was necessary to remove the desire of life.

They hit life up to its sources. They considered the union of the man and the woman as hateful and taught that marriage was guiltier than an illegitimate union because it was devoted by the company and by God and a permanent state of sin. For them, the sexual act of love had a power of appeal, a magical force of attraction which called a soul to life. The souls were enjoying a life of bliss and heavenly pleasure and men by copulating offered them by the material lust, a temptation of incarnation.

The natural consequence of the suppression of desire was the suppression of the life itself. They practiced suicide in all forms, but they had recognized and judiciously, that the most convenient way to die, with the view for the life of the afterlife was what they called the Endura. The Endura was to starve oneself to death. Sometimes it lasted long enough, because during the Endura, it was allowed to drink water. The lack of food caused a slow decay, similar to the one which gives a disease, favored the detachment from terrestrial things and thus allowed the dying to cross without a sudden shock, the threshold of death. We will see how this lack of shock has a utility.

It is in the history of the Albigensians, that one sees one of the most extraordinary examples of the power that nature instills to organiza-

---

* The most complete study on Albigensians is the one of Mr. Jean Guiraud in the first volume of the Cartulaire de Notre-Dame de Prouille. This is where are exposed most clearly the differences of the Albigensianism, Buddhism and Christianity. The impartiality of this presentation should also be noted.

tions when it wants them to survive and of the mysterious tenacity it brings to maintain certain forms predestined to live, for incomprehensible reasons.

A certain Guillelma of Toulouse, decided to die, opened her veins, thinking it was the fastest way to achieve her goal. No doubt, she did it clumsily, because she did it again several times. Continuing to live, she took to weaken herself, prolonged baths, which will perhaps fortify her unwittingly, because of the charity, unknown then, to hygiene. She took various poisons to which she resisted. As death did not come, she absorbed crushed glass to perforate her entrails. She was arrested and imprisoned as a heretic. She remained in prison a long time and her parents believed she was long dead when she reappeared, still alive. She had given up to die and abjured the Albigensian's heresy. A legend created around her, which said that death could not have a grip on her. She attained an extraordinary age. Her efforts had only served to give her some sort of physical eternity, which she did not want. As with love, there is no trifling with death.

The perfects of the Albigensian sect, that is to say those who had attained wisdom, were far from preaching the Endura as an obligation. The crowd of believers was only held to improve itself, to the extent of its forces, by living the life of everyone. The Endura was a sanctity sign among them and if there have been many Endura, it means that they included many saints. In exchange for life, the Albigensian faith opened to the one who was initiated, with the Consolamentum rite, a vast horizon of possibilities.

The Consolamentum was the seal of purification. The one who received it had confessed his sins. He had renounced them and the Consolamentum was the rite which erased their consequences, which removed the Karma. It was given by a Perfect and he had a kiss as symbol, because there cannot be a passport for the afterlife which is not marked with the sign of love. The Consolamentum contained a lost secret, transmitted by a forgotten word, it gave a revelation forever dead. It was the expression of the most divine magic, the one which allow to glimpse the reality of the spiritual life. Those who touched that reality wanted no more to participate to the reality which surrounded them. The Church saw that its sacraments were outdated. It understood the danger of this illuminating extreme unction and it decided to destroy it. It succeeded completely. The Albigensians were destroyers of the family and the society, as one had never seen before. It is because they possessed the secret of death and the one of the illuminated renaissance, that they were exterminated to the last.

The suicide of men and that of animals

Yet, whatever the disapproval which remains attached today to the idea of suicide, the suicide is not a human monstrosity. It is in nature, like a hidden force, expression of the eternal contradiction of life. If the vegetables do not commit suicide, which is not absolutely sure, there are numerous examples of animal suicides. Dogs commit suicide by starving to death, and this is what is best in them, the loyalty to a master who is dead, that is to say their own virtue in what higher it has, which drives them to this action. Some captive monkeys have acted the same, because they were deprived of the element by which they developed and which was liberty.

Not long ago, news papers have reported the suicide of a monkey in England, by hanging. I witnessed the suicide of a cat, and I had the feeling that an animal species manifested in this act, its nobility, that it elevated to a degree of intelligence, high enough to understand the misery by which it was struck and protested against this misery.

This female cat lived by the sea, with a fisher man, but she was regarding him only in a state of half servitude. She had a disease which made her limp and because of which she suffered. Her humor became taciturn. She had babies, but either by mistrust or by love of solitude, she carried them on a nearby hill, in the middle of savage heathers. One day, the fisher man was surprised to see her coming toward his house, followed by the little ones who were able to walk.

She took them to the foot of the man as for entrusting them to him., then she rushed deliberately towards the sea. The fisher man saw her going far enough among the waves where she struggled. He ran after her, pulled her out of the water and as he was attached to her, despite the oddity of her character, he wiped her, rubbed her and stretched her again on rags, in the sun. She let herself be pushed around but as soon as he left her, she rushed once again in the waves and this time, she went much further, and drowned.

Animal suffering is more mysterious than that of the man. The one who admires thoroughly the world's harmony explains the suffering in the human order as a mean given by God to progress or as the consequence of committed sins in successive lives. But what does he say about the hopeless suffering of the animal?

I looked at this place from the sea that the female cat had chosen to end her life. I remembered that Porphyry claimed that the psychic twin of an animal who died a violent death, does not get away from it and stands over it for a long time. I remembered also that students of death were unanimous in saying that the water was the the least proper element to separate the invisible body and that creatures that drowned had more difficulty than others to perform this necessary separation. I searched if some plaintive phosphorescence would indicate me the time of the evening, the place where stood the twin of a female cat who successfully overcame, by an unexpected act of freedom, all the instincts of the obscure animosity.

But that kind of research is always vain. The beast with tawny eyes of flame which had been wise enough to house his growing young against the cruelty of men, enough patience to wait for their forceful age, enough determination to secure the minute of his death, had made the atoms of his substance to the anonymous currents of the matter in motion. In the eternal transformations, there would be no evidence of its passage through the heathers of the hill and the sand from the beach. Intelligence and virtue of rank did not survive in duration. There was neither hope or perfection, nor promise of immortality for it. We know nothing of the soul of the beast and have never measured the radiance of its consciousness. Who knows if this perspective of nothingness had not confusingly appeared to it and had not helped to shorten its despair?

**

But suicide is a mistake of despair. Religions and systems of theosophy have banned it with threats and have exaggerated its dangers in a social and moral aim. Once the man pulled himself out, as he must always do, from the social and moral prejudices, he found himself in the case of suicide, in front of a danger more serious than that of pain, to which it is accustomed to by life.

The one who strikes his body with enough force to kill him, only destroys his physical body. He finds himself in the afterlife with the pain he wanted to escape and the causes of this pain. The violence of his action and the shock he received deprive him of sleep granted by nature after death or shorten this sleep. He wakes up with the anguish that required his action. Yet, he has no longer the same clear consciousness than the one of the time when he was still illuminated by the sun of the living. His anguish will continue without possible remedy to mitigate it.

If he committed suicide because of a disillusioned love, his disappointment will worsen in the afterlife because his love was the love of a form of flesh, and he will be in the world where forms are not even noticeable any more. He could have fed on earth a hope of reaching the beloved being, to conquer it by actions. But now he will not have the necessary form to action. If he killed himself out of fear and disgust of life, he will still have his fear and his disgust because he will not be aware enough to realize that where he is, he is delivered from evil and from the terrestrial ugliness. He will appear in the kingdom of shadows deprived of the essential element of all life, in any world, deprived of the luminous armor that everyone must forge by himself and which is the serenity of the joyous awareness. He risks, because of his weakness, to fall prey of the below larvae and of all the phantasmagoria of wandering desires and aborted imaginations.

Many saints of all religions, many ascetics have sought a temporary mean between suicide and natural death to flee life and attain faster the divine world. They exposed themselves to all weather, they offered their defenseless bodies to evil powers of diseases. This is a hypocritical form of suicide. The Church and the judgment of men also blinkered, beatify the crafty ones playing with the divine law and they refuse the holy land and the funeral honors to too sincere ones, to too violent persons who reject with too much abruptness, the fleshly form, mantle of the sin.

Moreover, nature gives reason to hypocrisy. Death by disease has envelopments and preparations which cover it if not smoothly, at least with indifference. The abrupt separation for the average man, is always accompanied by some pain. It causes inconsistency, it removes the return of consciousness, it aggravates the darkness.

***

One can commit suicide only among the greatest joy. It is necessary to have conquered joy, serene and definitive joy of intelligence and love, to give oneself voluntary death. Then the soul is detached from its earthly goods, it has molded itself the refined substance of the body where it will therefore live, it prepared its light, it can break the bond that unites it to the matter. But it is still necessary to have also developed in intelligence and love. And one still must be very advanced spiritually and must not leave home behind.

The absolute selfish, so high is its understanding, will not be guaranteed of an unexpected cold of solitude in the emotional world he penetrates. Similarly, the one who would be all love, but who would not possess the lamp of knowledge, would float in a soft wellbeing that the anguish of darkness would disturb.

The man who kills himself in perfect joy, soars far from the earthly world, as if he were launched by the force of his act and carried on a spiritual platform. But no one has the serenity that suits the audacity of separation. No man has in him a certainty strong enough about the afterlife and the least drop of doubt would be sufficient to mix with terror, the essential joy for the departure. No man has enough detachment, not even enough hope. All have too much obedience to the law.

And besides, it is much better. As soon as the list of conditions of superiority is enumerated, each, so poor he might be, thinks recognizing himself. If, by the sudden development of a belief like the one of Albigensians, suicide penetrated the customs, the most foolish would practice them first, vowing by pride and ignorance to sufferings after death and rapid returns on earth.

No one can easily escape to the form. It is not sufficient to destroy voluntarily our carapace of flesh, blood and bones in order to be delivered from it forever. The drunk who throws once his glass in disgust or fantasy is not delivered from his desire to drink. Suicide in most cases has an inverse effect of the one who one proposed and only fortifies the love for life. The one who wants to remove life must extract the perennial root, the fluid rope which joins it to the substance. Yet, the invisible root, more vigorous, more forked, more filled with thousands of rootlets than any other vegetable root, feeds on human seed, as the legendary mandrake. To destroy it, a secret of attractive order is needed. It is a key in the shape of a sex that opens the door of liberation.

The power of sexuality

Death is the path of the splendid life. But is can also lead to twilights of half unconsciousness.

All desires which are not feasible on the afterlife, desires which need matter to express themselves, become opaque mists when one is dead and prevents to move in the desirable light. The soul is like a lamp, which, at the same time as weak glimmer, produces familiar clouds of which it is veiled.

Ah! To rush with the joy of consciousness through the blue sky of the dead! How fast one must go and how far one must see! But the veil which do not allow clarity to pass, the living cloud which marks out all horizons is the one which is weaved with the sexual desire. It is by the sexual power that we are attached to the physical life and when we are called back on earth, it is by the vital need to be male or female in the flesh.

I am sure that as long as the sexual appeal will exist within me, I will be attracted towards incarnation to satisfy it. It will not be the curve of such arms particularly lukewarm, neither the expression of such face with split lips in offering, that will drive me towards earth.

It will be a force which will be part of the essence of my being and to which I will be forced to obey. I can feel this power inside me. I consolidated it through my existence and I am incapable of getting rid of it. It is not the result of my actions. Actions are poor creators. They imagine being important and only one thought well directed deletes their effects. The sexual root has been sunk within me by a daily thought. It has penetrated the narrow soil of my individual earth and I cannot extract it anymore.

With enough logic, I told myself for a long time that it was unimportant to perform an act which does not hurt anyone nor oneself. Yet, the physical act of love, not only does not hurt anyone, but causes sometimes pleasure to the two beings who practice it. It is in the apparent order of the world. It is the symbol of the higher principle of love, a sort of seal appended on the pact which is signed by two united creatures.

I was wrong. I did not take into account the magical character of this act. I still ignored that when it does not engender, physically, small beings having a human form, it produces in the invisible world, procreations all the more numerous that there are fewer births of small beings.

The only sexual desire fed by the solitary thought, emits forces which take a confused existence and which react on us. The people of these creations accompany us, lives in our atmosphere, walks with us, feeds of our substance and gives us back, by a continual exchange, what we have given to it. Sometimes, in a fever state, we manage to perceive the strange forms to which we granted the existence.

I was able to realize it, in the clairvoyance which favored the onset of the disease.

It began by geometrical signs. Triangles first passed in large numbers. They were followed by lively quadrangles and circles whose whirling, fast at first, gradually slowed. A point appeared in the middle of these circles and this point became an eye, a blinking eye, devoid of intelligence, particularly fixed. Then geometric figures vanished to make way to forms. These forms had a singular ability of lengthening. They were half-animal, half-human, they stretched like clouds, fell like folds of cloth, had appearances of bodies. Their face, instead of occupying a normal place, was either on the back or on the chest or at the juncture of the legs and the mouth was often confused with a female sex.

I was lying on a low bed, I possessed or felt to possess all the lucidity of my mind and the forms were moving around me, in the light that half-closed curtains allowed to pass. I observed them with attention.

They became more and more alive and I noticed that they seemed conducted by a coupling desire. They moved closer to one another and merged and as the unions of these larvae took place, the figures became more alive, more human and imprinted of an expression which was neither good nor evil, neither love nor hatred, but an impersonal envy of sexual satisfaction. I think I have never seen something more implacable, fiercer, than those figures with dead eyes, moving mouths, which reflected no feeling, only a longing for sexes dilatation, of blind copulations.

These ghostly larvae stretched with a helpless enjoyment of sadness and they fell on me. My bed was covered with a yellow quilt that seemed to drink them like a sponge and became, in a few minutes, a receptacle of mated shapes, of ephialtes in fermentation. The quilt, with its folds, favored the slow grimacing faces. The outlines were becoming more precise and were sometimes so haunting and of an obscenity so bewildering that I stretched out my hand to a cane that was in a corner of the room and with which I could hit right and left, change the undulations of the quilt, where contortions rolled out and were the hugging took place.

No figure was complete, no member had an appearance of perfection. I saw deformed beings who were all unknown to me. Some had a particular personality, but none reminded me of a character once met, none had the attitude of a woman who already rested against me. All did not look like the absolute insensitivity, the native baseness and a strange tendency to develop in seconds disproportionate sexes.

Striking with my cane the faces which turned towards me and considered me with too much attention, hustling on the quilt cloudy breasts, the larval torsos, brought down the prominence of appendices, I wondered anxiously from where these ever seen creatures came from. Ever seen, certainly! And yet, wasn't there, in these void expressions, something that was familiar to me? In some nocturnal dreams, hadn't I glimpsed similar obscenities?

And suddenly, the light dawned on me. I understood.

These independent beings attracting each other, these incomplete monsters which took their beats around my fever, it was me who had put them in the world. They were the offspring of my dreams. They were myself. If bad father a man may be, he remains in the dependence of his sons. Thus, I was condemned to be followed by those lower companions. I had created and I depended on them. They radiated currents running through my bleak. I had to look at myself. These horrific images were the projection of my soul. The day I will enter the kingdom of the afterlife, and where I will find myself in the presence of a fraternal spirit, if he asked me: What did you do during your life? I would not need to answer. He would see me in the middle of the monsters I had patiently bared.

I gently placed the cane at the foot of my bed and I kept my eyes closed for a long time.

***

I have long found the monsters charming and I enjoyed their company. I knew, from my youth, that the intelligence is the real purpose of life, but I thought it was possible to do two parts: that of pleasure and of the mind. I told to myself that a tamer, between the sessions where he enters in the cages of his menagerie, has time to read Plato and learn the doctrine of the Buddha. I did not think that many members of Pezon and Bidel families had been eaten by their big cats.

The bodies of the monsters I created cannot be pierced by the trident of the tamer and if I give them lashes, they expand and grow.

Some apprentices in wisdom who have found themselves facing the same problem as I, tried to solve it by a method of gratification. With sincerity, they have engaged in all sensual satisfactions to attain satiety. I think they only arrived to a natural satiety. However, their method is less dangerous than the one of saints and ascetics. It is perhaps more enjoyable. Saint Anthony's temptations were told by the poets as much as by mystical writers. They are the history of all those trying recklessly to be chaste. One might as well try to live without eating or drinking.

The ancient wisdom of India prescribed to the average man, a significant rule of life. Youth should be dedicated to activity and pleasure. In the middle of the existence, the man was supposed to start a family, and have children. Approaching an old age, he was supposed to retire in a forest to meditate there the advice of nature, learn the sublime message transmitted by birds and find in his heart the light which hides there.

But this wisdom is hardly valid in the West. First, there cannot be rules for the average man. We have developed pride to that point that as soon as a man has moved two or three ideas, he consider himself as superior and outside of humanity. It is true that in the cases, infinitely rare, of superiority, another rule would be necessary. If one imagines a community bringing together both Plato, Plotinus, Goethe and Spinoza, each, whatever his culture, would blame them of dedicating the maturity of their life to give birth to a large number of children.

Furthermore, the Hindu rule cannot be applied among us because there is no forest where the aging man eager for wisdom can retire. Our society is so poorly made and men are so bad that the poor is despised by his poor brothers and looked at the rich look at him with a condescension more odious than contempt. The wise, sitting in the shade of a pin would not spend a day without a police officer asking for his papers and without an honest worker spiting on him because he is idle. The rudeness and hatred would envelop him and would poison the purity of his meditations.

***

How to behave then regarding this inner force which brings us eternally into the circle of forms and of the physical enjoyment.

All that exists is likely to transform either by spiritualizing and rising by one degree, either going backwards. There are two possibilities in the physical love of a man and a woman. But the power of making gold is attributed to few being s and the alchemy that uses human sexes to undertake the great work is particularly difficult. It is the one where the invisible ingredients should be dosed as delicately as possible. This is where the visible ingredients have the most formidable effects. And often when the alchemist is delighted because he believes that the operation has succeeded, only means that he has killed in himself the ability to distinguish the pure gold of the raw material.

This secret should be known and practiced in the temples of Greece where the cult of Venus was celebrated, that is to say of the attractive power. For the Greeks, there were two Venuses, the vulgar and physical Venus, and the spiritual Venus. The schools of priestesses which were in the same time schools for courtesans, appeared to our ignorant minds of having only been ashes of debauchery. The vulgar Venus asked the study of resources delivered by the body for the delight and searched for means to multiply this delight by the art of caresses. But in the cult of the spiritual Venus, had to be taught, the path of the spiritualization by the physical pleasure.

Religious secrets of love were not fixed by the writing on parchment, nor engraved on stone. They are now lost. Beauty gestures and movements of pleasure have been diverted of the mind. Yet, the principle perishes, if one cease to believe in it. No temple is higher than love.

The love that can make us the equals of the gods, has been deprived of its sublime privilege and it is now only glorified for the generation. One only respects in it its lowermost function. And those who would want to find the lost secret must do it obscurely, without the help of any tradition and with all the risks that this search comprises.

The spasm of love and the one of death

There is a mystery in the spasm of physical love. Perfect equilibrium between suffering and joy, it is only tolerable in our blinkered organism for few seconds. It is an foretaste of the creative joy that we will know in a way, if not permanently, at least infinitely sustainable, when we will covered by a more perfect body. Nature wanted the operation to create to put, for a second, the creator in the divine plan.

There is an intimate link between the spasm of love and the one of death. Both are the symbol of a communication with a higher state. But the communication of death is passive, the one of love is active.

The joining of the two spasms is the highest sensation to which man can claim. Certain lovers suffering from a heart disease have known it. It is attributed to those who die by hanging. But neither the lovers, nor the hanged ones, have the necessary knowledge to take a sublime advantage of the coincidence of the two spasms. Those who have fully enjoyed it, had incidentally neither the power nor the desire to relate it.

As well as the view of a billionaire who gives a penny to a poor provokes indignation, and then burst out laughing, as one must laugh at the monstrous avarice of nature that has given so few moments to the divine enjoyment of the spasm. But whatever its desperate brevity, one should consider the spasm as a lightning, revealing lighthouse that provides a glimpse into a dazzling glow, the horizon of another cosmic plan.

Sometimes, at night, in a hotel room, a strange complaint can be heard. First, one thinks that there is somewhere a suffering creature, but gradually one has the perception of a regular panting, and the moaning voice seems to come out of another world. It seems that the room, separated from the room where one is, by a partition, which trembles, is located in another planet. The moaning creature has temporarily left the terrestrial world that once confined to her, drawn curtains, shriveled carpets, anonymous walls. She is in the universe of the spasm, universe which opens and closes as rapidly as an image seen in a dream.

Everyone participates for few seconds to the life of this universe. Each receives differently its revelation. Very few uses the light received from it. Each can measure his dose of animosity and the dose of disgust that the end of the spasm leaves to him.

The disgust is the assured sign that the pleasure has demeaned you instead of raising you. Every man had sometimes felt the call of the beast after love. Two people who communicate with joy in the pleasure cannot create disgust, because they exchanged between them subtle forces. The exchange is physical as well as moral and it enriches. The embrace or love is reciprocal and causes so to speak, no tiredness of the body.

Thus can be measured the sincerity of the gift in love. And there is also no sadness. Joy, when the spasm has just expired, is the sign of the chosen ones.

Men willing to rise towards spirituality have thought to transform into mind the sexual elements. The principle is to dematerialize the spermatic essence and to transform them into subtler atoms that strengthen the spiritual body. It is a higher alchemy which formula remained secret. It is not known if some sage achieved this goal. But there must be sudden returns of the irritated sexuality being transformed, because one can see sometimes men who have lead for a long time a too perfect life, seized suddenly by a desire of violence without measure. The desire comes back then, deformed, abnormal and furious, as if it wanted to take revenge on the compression it had suffered.

It is more prudent to use the physical love in order to rise in the spiritual order, without trying to destroy it, but by practicing it with measure and adoration and by considering it even as a sacrament.

It is not necessary to give it the value of a ceremony. The desire of senses is brutal and it appears suddenly. One might even say that it has a certain independence in the human organism. It does not obey to the drive. He refuses any regulations. One cannot call it at any hour of the day. One must await its good pleasure. It wakes you up sometimes in the middle of the night and makes you do reckless actions. In reality, it is submitted to currents we ignore the origin and of which an astrology very sophisticated could indicate us the passages and the disappearances.

As a plant one waters, the sensual desire grows as one satisfies it, and if one does not satisfy it, it dives deep roots in us, difficult to extract. It is, in short, like a fool who goes from right to left, that comes, then goes back and engages in a thousand follies. One must seize this madman, this autonomous visionary, and while appearing to satisfy his whims, steer him in a new direction, giving its actions a religious significance.

This religiosity has no rite and no ceremonial. It consists in enjoying the spasm of love to enrich one's soul and conquer by it a power which will cross death. Each celebrates in its own way the sexual mystery. Greeks and Romans had recognized that the love practiced collectively had a greater impact. They did not only think of the increase of the delight. They thought with reason that by the mean of the spasm it was possible to create a more complete union that the one of two beings, the union of an entire group. A powerful collective entity could have arisen in this way. Perhaps they have realized, but it degenerated rapidly in vulgar debaucheries which produced the opposite effect. Because if the physical love has the power to rise, it is only in some cases and its lowering power is much greater. It would be in vain, in the miserable times we live in, to make an attempt of that order. It is already very difficult to be two.

But when the number of two is attained, those who want to derive the greatest benefit from love, need to think that their mutual desire of union is the vital element. Some perfumes can be aids, also the blending of incense and musk. One should avoid the contact with metals, even jewelry and especially the contact with gold which stores continuously the desires of which it is the object. One should not have drunk alcohol which paralyses in the organism, the birth of spiritual affinities. Perhaps, but with great precautions, one will be able to use opium which favors the gift of oneself, to someone one loves. The hand which ceases the neck, where the hair arises, will contribute to the exchange of affectionate currents. United spirits will be the symbol of the union subtler of the essences of being.

And when lovers will feel things shirking around them, when the approach of the spasm will throw them in this disorder that changes the sound of the voice and gives the cry of pleasure the tone of despair, they will have to, despite the veil which falls on the soul, create an inner image, a living image of themselves. That with the best possible sharpness they represent to themselves their two beings united, melted into one single ideal and spiritualized creature. When the spasm will make pass in their body its metal molten stream, they will glimpse, within a second, a door opened to the world of the afterlife. That the double image which became unique rushes through that door to appear during an infinitesimal bit of time in the unknowable region. This fleeting creature, this girl with an imaginative affection, will fall with the end of their pleasure, will vanish like the warmth of their kiss, will let them both again and separated in the bed that became deeper. But she would have presented herself on the divine threshold as the testimony of their terrestrial contribution, of what best a man and a woman can accomplish, the ultimate and perfect creation of their love.

Perfection through love

Doctors have told me that sometimes were brought in hospitals, men, marked by the fatal sign of solitude. Questioned on the address of their families, they answered that all their relatives were dead since a long time. They had no wife, no mistress, no friend. No one was interested in their fate. And if one insisted, they eventually indicated as the being that was closest to them, the tenant of the lodging-house where they were struck by the disease.

No state seemed to me more miserable that the one of the loners who went through life without creating a link which united them to their siblings. Did this solitude come from a native egoism, from a hubris? Had they caused it by their lack of love or had they been hit by a combination of circumstances? What would happen to those, the minute after death? Would they compensate this infinite misery of loneliness? How could they benefit from the effects of causes that they had not created?

And I thought that all the life of men is a fight against solitude. They gather in families, they press in cities, they become attached to one another to escape the terrible immensity of the universe, to the formidable perspective of being face to face with themselves.

But whatever the effort that everyone does, his selfishness is so powerful, his thoughts and actions are so naturally directed towards him, that he goes in life almost lonely, lonelier than he can imagine, in his most pessimistic meditations.

It is a melancholic experience to do than ask his friends to what number they set, in all sincerity, beings who are strongly attached to them, strongly enough to have shaken their existence if they were to die. One must of course exclude of that list his father and mother. It is oneself, his physical extension that a man loves in his child. That love is the most selfish of all because it reports directly to our instincts. The conditions are more noble as they escape the bonds of blood and are the result of choice.

Those who are questioned first believe they can include a high number of beings of which they have the love. But they realize on reflection that these loves are often appearances of love based on the interest that one has to love and that the removal of the interest would result in the removal of love. Having speculated and added, the optimists find two, sometimes three names. Most of them realize sadly that they must be very happy if there is one creature on earth that loves them with sincerity and selflessness.

A creature, only one! And yet it may die, or, worst case, to stop loving you. Love is the greatest wealth, and after having reached out its hands, desired, having given himself with all the heart, this is the man's harvest!

This inconceivable poverty, this unprecedented misery is due to the initial mistake of the purpose of our affections. We restricted our love to mankind. And in humans we also restricted it to a being with a different sex with whom we take pleasure.

The love for plants and minerals, the planets and the light is of the same essence as the other loves to which it agreed to give respect. It should be taught in schools and the methods that develop it should be popularized. I have often wondered by what unforgivable oblivion or what incredible ignorance, Jesus Christ had restricted his prescriptions of love to men's love for each other. A single word of the Gospels on our relationship with the animals would have saved millions of creatures, would have decreased for centuries the ferocity of the human species.

For there is only one quality of love and no matter how one develops it. The famous benefactors, creators of great works, are not superior to those who are doomed to a modest daily donation. A sage sitting in a field, who would devote himself to the happiness of an ant, would obey to its insect requirements, would accomplish his long journeys with his fingertip, would be the conqueror of wealth as great as the pastor of man whose effort would feed the people. No matter to what or whom we give ourselves. It is the gift of oneself that is essential.

Insofar as one has practiced this gift on earth, one has a largest wellness after death. Because one has complied in advance with the new law. The being in the current which carries him, towards birth, goes to the condensation and selfishness. In the one who wins it by death, he goes to the expansion, the communication with the universe.

***

— Perfection is acquired by the possession of a lover, according to his soul, said Plato.

The most sublime purpose of life is to find a lover according to his soul. But what a task a how delicate!

How to recognize him among so many faces? And if one thinks he recognized him, how to guarantee if it is not a mistake? So many pitfalls that stop you in this pursuit! One gives you all the fun you can have, but his betrayal disappoints you. Another comes with moral qualities similar to yours, but it is then a physical misunderstanding that draw him away from you. Pleasure is a guide sometimes, and other times it is a misleader that fools you with a kiss.

According to Plato, perfect lovers are two halves, the active and the passive principle which once formed a single whole. This unified whole was separated by the incarnation, but the two halves aspire to join and find their true nature which is to be one.

Nature uses the same laws by transposing them. As an author who, for lack of imagination, repeats the same effects in a play, thus the divine uses in all stages of its creation, a similar mechanism. "The protozoa multiply by division of a mother cell into two daughter cells*."

But in order not to grow old and die, they must come together again and "become two in one by a kind of sexual union." The law of the human soul is similar. There was division. It is necessary to become once more two in one. The universal key of all thing is hidden in this essential law of both male and female principles.

So there would be on earth only one being with whom one could accomplish his divine realization. Yet, if virtuous characters and are favored by luck find at the beginning of their life this half and live with

* Henry de Varigny, *La mort et la biologie.*

her an entire existence in happiness, there are others who find it and then realize, by horrible character differences or cynical dropouts, that they made a mistake. There are others who, after long years of passionate and mutual love, lose the loved one by death. They experience a short but endless despair and they meet a new loved one they love of a love as passionate and as mutual. One can mention rich souls through the attraction and the gift of themselves, which four and even five times in their lives met with divine halves. If one questions them, they cannot designate between these beloved creatures, which one was the truly complementary double of their soul, always eager to possess.

The love of two beings for one another is a way to reach the divine. The love for the stones, plants or gods, are other paths. The key is to take one, no matter which one. The one taken by lovers is the most human. The momentum of all the forces of the world goes to their meeting, to their return to unity. Two beings who align their bodies along with their ideal aspirations, achieve a partial unit, starts the work of nature.

This work must be realized the more easily one tries it, with the most fraternal companion, the being one found most frequently in the course of his existence. Two lovers united voluntarily, through the good and evil they reciprocally make to each other, work to a perfection. They build their unity. They mingle intimately by their love until they spiritually combine, what appears to be the supreme purpose of the spirit, at least the one which is given to us to observe, as far as our sight can go.

When they harmoniously get to complement, the desire of the flesh may no longer downgrade them. It is nothing more than the sign of their possession, the physical interpretation of a higher state. Then, they can escape to the reincarnative power. Having focused on themselves all their desires and all their aspirations, the call of earthly life no longer exists for them. What drags the others towards the physical life only pushes them to themselves, towards a more complete realization of their unity. Having become absolutely inaccessible to the terrestrial call, they can be projected into the post-human state, because they have created an entity too powerful to be imprisoned in a body as those one sees on earth.

Naturally, this result is infinitely rare. Beings who love each other are almost all condemned to separation. They know the pain of changing form one before the other, to call each other in vain on the inaccessible shores of different worlds, to reach out their invisible hands, without knowing whether they will be able to find one day, the only warmth that is worth facing the inexorable misery of living.

The infidelity of the deceased

Those who loved each other meet again. There is no coalition of Gods, no cosmic power which can prevent this meeting. Creative moons of humid chaos, crazy suns, do not have the capacity to break the affinity of two beings determined to join after the transformations of death. These two beings cannot be separated by nothing, neither by the long years which traverse the one who is abandoned alone in life, whereas the other, wanders in the afterlife, neither by the posthumous sleeps even more longer, by nothing — if it is not the power of memory lapse which is in both of them.

Yet, the joining only exists in virtue of the spiritual character of love and it has opportunities all the greater of duration that this love has been less material.

Death destroys the form, the beloved form which has been the interpreter of our happiness and the crucible of our suffering. Death makes resonate to our ear an inexorable never again.

Never again will the eyes shine, these lamps where appeared the kindness of the soul, never again will the hands quake, these agile aids of pleasure, never again will the chest pulsate where one put one's forehead. "What once has changed of form, will never take it back again in the infinity of duration".

In degree of development of the man, love is especially a love of the form. The pleasure plays a dominating role and the body is the instrument of pleasure, that is to say of what is the most important in life.

One can hardly imagine the existence of someone one loves deprived of the body in which one was used to see him. Many loves did not resist to the ordeal of a body change.

Religions and philosophies have understood the desire of men of being perpetuated in their flesh and they have searched means more or less possible to satisfy this desire. Because religions and philosophies are like governments, they seek to satisfy human wishes. Instead of teaching what they know of the truth, they veil this truth if it is cruel, and they instruct theories in relation to the aspirations of majorities. The resurrection of bodies is in the Mazdeism. Kabbalah speaks of the spirit of the bones which is an invisible physical seed keeping the model of the body. Saint Paul assumes that a mysterious seed survives to the destroyed being and that men will come back to life in their flesh at the time of the last judgment. Nowadays, Charles Renouvier admits "the existence of an invisible organism which survives to the sensitive body and keeps the required powers to produce a form of body similar or higher than the one it already put on". He adds, it is true, without irony, "that this hypothesis is all the stronger as one explains it less".

The dogma of the resurrection of bodies, under any form whatsoever, do not resist to the test of a reasonable mind. The forms of flesh are dissolved in all tombstones. By the bye we make during our lifetime, the experience of the death of the bodies. Our form is in a state of constant changing and the one of the old man has no common molecule with the one of the ancient young men he once was.

But from the deformed statue, form the image which betrayed itself, remains the memory that each keeps one. The memory is the defense of the man against the devouring principle of time, against the force of changes.

The greatest risk for those who love each other is to have a too great separation of years between the moments of their death. We see that the one of the two who stays alive, often forgets by the game of life, and its new attractions, the one he has lost. But the danger of oversight comes especially of the one which is death. Nature has spread in the currents of the afterlife; the invisible floods of the Lethe so that the deceased water their without knowing it. On the shores of this river lined with poppies, they walk in a dream state and with the appearance of their empty hands, they take this water of the color of sleep. This oversight granted to the dead is the most divine gift of nature.

The dead who loved is forced to defend his love against himself with more ardor than the one who stayed on earth. He is forced to perpetuate by the memory an image which will have less chance to be real in him, as it will transform on earth and will cease to correspond to reality. This fight for the memory is favored for the dead by the terrestrial atmosphere of the one he loves; in which he will try to remain. He must resist to the intoxicating temptation of the confuse dreams, the transformative dreams. And his victory is of course proportioned to his degree of consciousness.

Whatever the love that these two beings think they have for each other, if they are separated for long, they risk not to find in themselves the harmony which once made their happiness. This harmony was an ability to vibrate together and to give the same resonances. The harmony when they will meet again can be different. The man transforms in the hard condensation of his physical form. We are, during our lifetime, melancholic witnesses of it. But how he transforms more easily when his form became subtler! The one who dies first, becomes by its own nature, more likely to changes. The curiosity for the new world where he finds himself, the game of his own thought which arise continuously his ability of penetration, will push him if he reaches a certain development, to travel through the endless horizons, placed before him. How will he resist to the marvelous enjoyment that will procure him his new ability of expansion?

The deceased are strangely unfaithful, more unfaithful that the living. And they are all the more since they have attained a greater development. The average man who only possess in the afterlife a confused consciousness can easily remain focused on the terrestrial attraction of the one he loved. Within the dream in which he baths, he finds a languor full of well-being. He does not distinguish any other possibility than this tepid warmth of affection. He rests and waits. His fidelity is all the more certain as he does not perceive the temptations of his new life.

But if death is developed in knowledge, whether physical desires do not darken his vision, it will be different. The earth will appear to him in its true colors, as a deprived planet, a center of pain with a dark purple color, around which turn the most material currents of the creation. He will understand the formidable impact of this original fall, always poorly explained and always misunderstood. He will glimpse the worlds of the spirit where, in a state of subtler matter, drifts the archetypes of beauty of which all he had known on earth was only the miserable caricature.

He will have to love then, not to try to break forever the bonds that hold the universe in pain! It is only insofar as the loved one he has left on earth will become a part of himself, that he will remain attached to it. The more temptation is spiritual, the more powerful it is*.

The lovers that death separates have a double fight to support in different world, to keep to one another. The confused perspective of the danger of oversight has often pushed those who loved each other to die together. They fully benefit then from the force of their creation. One might say that they rise higher, by remembering that it is not a height in space. The most intelligent or the one who has more love, seeing more clearly, clears for the other, the darkness. Solitude is vanquished and according to the mutual balance of their terrestrial desires, they will perhaps triumph of the reincarnation.

But death in common is rare and the mean of suicide of the one who stays is full of uncertainties and dangers. It is wiser for those who love each other to get used to, during their lifetime, a fidelity that will exceed the threshold of death. By habit, this thought will fortify, will become inherent to the soul, to the point that one will be not able to imagine a spiritual enjoyment that is not shared. The chain that reunites the lovers becomes alive, it is like a luminous river through which circulates, from one to the other, the divine water of the mind.

Death does not interrupt this communication. It withstands years. And when those who have been separated, even for a long time, find each other again, they see each other, they hug with the appearance of their best days, the best days of their love. Because they find each other again in a world where thought is creative, where it is the reality. By the power of the memory, they mutually create their image and they enjoy the presence of this beloved form, all the more real that it is imagined.

---

* A spirit communication wrote down in the interesting work of Mr. CORNILLIER, *The Survival of the Soul*, gives reason to what I say. A spirit of higher order can be seen, which does not even recognize with whom he was very close during his lifetime.

The inner spirit of the truth

I thank the order of things, the distributive law which give birth to one with a ridiculous nose and the other with a faculty of stoutness, for giving me the knowledge of death. I thank this miserly law for being generous for once by giving me not only the knowledge of death but the inner certainty of truth. Because there are people who know, who expose their science with seriousness, but who draw no joy from it, because deep within them they do not believe. I thank the distributive law by which few souls are covered by the ulcer of the doubt, of having made me believe in what I thought.

Often, by reading books of men who have dealt with what happens after death, and who made it with meticulous details, I laughed at their pretention or according to my humor, I outraged myself because they did not provide the proof of their affirmations. And now I am tempted to do the same. But what proof can I provide to the others, that are different from the one that I have given o myself?

I have heard that there was in India, few years ago, a local judge, an old judge animated by a sense of justice, who by dint of meditating on the truth and on the lie of testimonies, recognized, with a particular sense, what was true and what was false. His particular sense must have been based on face expressions, on intonations of voices.

Am I too arrogant by comparing myself to this local judge? I had, at a certain time, the perception that a new sense appeared within me and developed with progress quite sensitive. This sense manifested by a light inner suffering, when, during a conversation or when reading a book related to the subject which interested me between all, I found myself in the presence of an idea, opposite to the truth.

As the Hindu judge, I meditated on the descriptions of the future life, on the dreams of the clairvoyant, on the assertions of spiritualists. Very often, I felt the little inner pain, sign of the presence of the lie and I noticed that it was proportional, not to the grandeur of the lie, but the will of falsity that had the speaker of the lie. The pure error, the incredible error accomplished by ignorance or stupidity, instead of causing myself suffering, provoked within me a happy laugh, this joy that causes deformation of the comic.

I listened an advice that was formulated without a word and I was rewarded for my attention. Thus I learned with certainty the part of the truth there was in ancient traditions, I knew in what measure one had to add faith to the extravagant imaginations of the seers who claimed to converse directly with God. No doubt that each man can develop this inner sense and perhaps is this a modest beginning of communication with the so-called God. I thank the distributive law that grants one an abundant ability to enjoy the taste and touch, obviating others by the delicate antennae of sympathy, for giving me a small part of discernment in the field of what is hidden.

I do not envy the seers who have astonished the world by their clairvoyance. They have seen too much in my opinion. The lie has always a weak point by which it betrays itself. The pure imagination eventually burst like a soap bubble that reflected too many rainbows.

The ancient revelations of the Vedas of India are broken by too many offering demands for the Brahmins, authors of those revelations. Visions of catholic saints representing God exclusively surrounded by catholic saints, which makes the vision fade. Many times, by reading books where related communications made with all the desirable controls, I was filled by amazement. But I always stumbled over few stones which made me fall from the top of my credulity.

I successively red two works where life of the men in the afterlife was described, according their good or bad nature, in an almost similar way. This concordance came to support the veracity of these Spiritualists experimenters. But I was surprised that both assigned a particularly happy and high place to the soldiers who died for their country. I do not believe that the afterlife has similar rewards to our titles and our decorations and I think that those who die in the violence, by killing their fellows, even if it is for the country, suffer the backlash of violence which is always painful. My astonishment was dissipated when I saw that the authors of these two sincere books, and to some extent, scientists, were both colonels, one in the French army, the other in the English army.

— I had the opportunity to be with the angels and talk with them as a man with another man and that for thirteen years now, said Swedenborg.

I could not help myself but to envy Swedenborg. I also envied the theosophist Leadbeater and anthroposophist Rudolf Steiner. These are those who went the farthest in the affirmation of an almost miraculous clairvoyance. Swedenborg has made a meticulous description of the underworld. He lies it in the mountains and he noticed that their entries "sometimes spacious were most of the time rugged." He saw fights, thefts and many places of debauchery*.

Leadbeater describes the afterlife as a kind of terrestrial counterfeit. There are bookstores, shops. Since few living have, like him, the ability to go there, when he takes walks there, one recognized him because his silhouette is familiar. One surrounds him, and asks him news about earth.

Steiner was able to follow the man after his death in his six-time journey through the planets†. He could go back in time, witness the creation of worlds, see the spaces when the earth was not born yet, when the sun had not yet taken shape. I followed him with passion. But there came a time when I cried out: "This is too much! How was he able to see so far? Where was he able to find these almost divine powers?" Yet, to these legitimate questions that any reasonable man must have asked him, and must have asked himself, he never answers. He even published a book of memoirs in which he notifies incidentally, his gifts of clairvoyance, without thinking to explain how they came!

There is among the seers a thrill of clairvoyance that merges with the imagination. They are carried away by the temptation that creates their desire to see what no one has seen. They portray with vivid colors fictions that are within them. And they swim, full of certainty, in an ideal dream which is true for them. When they have reached a certain degree, they are not embarrassed by anything. The good and evil ap-

---

* SWEDENBORG, *Heaven and its Wonders and Hell from Things Heard and Seen.*
† Rudolf STEINER, *Life after death.*

pears to them as well-defined plains, separated by a sparkling river like a sword. At the right everything is pure and white, on the left are the shadows of evil. And in this naive conception of property that is closely their personal property of an evil that is what is wrong with their eyes, lies the touchstone of their truth and their lies.

Ah! I wish I had the chance to talk to the angels for thirteen years, as Swedenborg! Even one familiar angel would have been enough for me. I would have liked my silhouette to be known in the afterlife, my name to be called by someone, one asking me questions, as it happened to Leadbeater! Also as Steiner, I would have liked to see the work of the Exusiaï, the Dynamis, the Kyriotetes, creative entities working on future human destinies! Yet, I thank the distributive law, which only attributed me an inner spirit, a small and modest guide, but which is in accordance with my reason.

It is by listening the silent word of this guide that I could transmit a message regarding death.

The scale, the monster, and the bridge

The deceased must be weighted in a scale! The deceased must cross a bridge! The deceased must fight a monster and perhaps be devoured by it! What is this scale, what is this bridge, what is this monster, that can be found in all primitive faiths and which are the symbol of an ordeal?

— My shadow should not be retained! Is written in the Egyptian *Book of the Dead*.

The shadow can be retained and this in virtue of a judgment and the judgment is pronounced in virtue of a certain weight of the soul in a mysterious scale.

The Egyptians represented the judgment with an astonishing solemnity. It took place before Osiris, radiating by sunlight. At the time when the deceased left his heart on one of the pans, Anubis, with a jackal head, put on the other pan a statuette of the goddess of justice. Horus, with a sparrow hawk's head, verified the weight with an acute eye which made any fraud impossible. Thoth, with an ibis' head, the God of writing, court clerk full of attention, inscribed on a shelf, the result of the weighing. And forty-two judges corresponding to forty-two capital sins pronounced in an inexorable way.

The ceremony of the judgment is simplified in other religions, but is found in all of them. The men have an innate need to be judged and punished. There is for them no possible existence without punishment*. And among all peoples, one attains the formidable presence of the judges only after terrible adventures, in religions filled with darkness and

---

* One is surprised to see this idea of judgment persist in a childish way, among some modern oculists. Mr. Sédir claims that at the time of death, one is suddenly surrounded by two spirits which lead one in front of a court chaired by Jesus Christ. Yet, Jesus Christ is not always present in this court. Mr. Lancelin imagines a strong form of punishment. The animals to whom a man has systematically harmed during his life, will, at the time of death, wait for him at his way out of the physical plan and take revenge on his astral body.

stench. Woe to he who has forgotten to take under his arm the Book of the Dead or who do not know the sentences! He loses his way through bayou where float poisonous mists, he falls into spiral chasms, he is surrounded by grimacing creatures. Mexicans killed a dog to accompany the deceased and guide him with its dog's flair through the backwaters, the lifeless forests, the twilight valleys. Among certain peoples of Oceania, as the journey must have been exhausting, it was preferable to die in the prime of life in order to have the necessary strengths to face it. Pious children killed their parents before their bodies were weakened.

But after the formidable religions where the traveler, whatever his resistance and his dog's flair, has all the chances to lose himself, there is a bridge to cross. The Mazdéits call it Tchinwat and it leads to the paradise of Ormuzd. Muslims call it Essirat and they say that it is more fine than a hair and more sharp than a sharpened sword. The just cross it a single momentum, with the rapidity of lightning, but the wicked slips there and are rushed in scholarly and numerous overlays of hells. The Algonquins had imagined that the bridge was made of thin intertwined snakes whose hissing gave dizziness.

And to cross this bridge, one must fight a monster and sometimes several monsters. The sight of it is so terrible that sometimes it is sufficient to make the man renounce and make him go backwards. Sometimes it is a monkey, sometimes a crocodile, sometimes the gathering of monkeys and crocodiles. It is sometimes a dog, often a snake, often a dragon, it is the Cerberus of the Greeks.

The great ordeal of the afterlife is the one of the lost intelligence than one must rediscover. After the sleep that the shock of death determines, the man wakes up. He is then lost. He does not know where he is anymore and what surrounds him, perhaps compared to darkness. To pierce this darkness, he makes the effort to which he is accustomed in such cases, the effort of the outward direction. And this effort is useless. It is within his soul that he will find the opportunity to see. But he does not know that. It is then that he has the feeling of traveling in these endless regions. His fear and confused recollections lend itself to what surrounds him of the appearances of frightening landscapes of which horizons are endless. He will sometimes have the feeling to travel underground

halls. Other times, he will see arise in front of him mountains he will be surprised to cross as easily as a fog. These landscapes will gradually disperse, making way to a confused twilight created by his thought and which will meet more light as he has within him the substance of its brightness. It is in this light, very vague for some, which will be able to be dazzling for others, that he will see himself, that he will contemplate the unfolding of his life, his thoughts, his actions, their causes and their consequences, what he knows and what he is.

It is then that he will leave his heart on the pan of the scale. He will weight himself. He will be the forty-two judges of the court. He will be all the sovereign gods. His sight will be more acute that if he wore the head of an sparrow hawk. He will inscribe with more care than if he had an ibis leg, the enumeration of his sins, or rather what he considers as being his sins. He will be clairvoyant, inexorable, generator of his own justice. Because in this solemn minute of judgment, as if he was penetrated of a swift cosmic lightning, he will see his relationships with other men, and the creatures of other reigns, he will see what is his acquired intelligence, his lot of love, the residue of his life. He will judge himself with a rigorous mathematics, according to the measure of possibilities he had had, and of which he has more or less served well. And if he does not possess then a higher wisdom which allows him, as by a magical operation, to burn the wastes of his existence, he will condemn himself. Of that condemnation will arise the monster.

The monster will cross him with the bite of the obsession. He will have the teeth of a crocodile, the ears of a donkey, the sex of a goat according to whether he will be the remorse of cruelty, ignorance and lust. The monster is the obsession which devours and which forces one to restart continuously, by the thought, the actions that one has accomplished and one would rather not have accomplished. The monster is the reverse of his own life, the double of himself, the force contrary to the mind. The man fights hand in hand with the monster and the fight is either long or short, according to whether he expands, to press, the claws of memories, depending on whether the man go through it with the sword of knowledge.

One can have an idea more or less exact of this state by what happens sometimes to one during certain nights. One wakes up suddenly and one is the prey of a forgotten regret, of the memory of an action one has made, or one should have made. This memory relies on two or three other accessory ideas and their gathering forms a chain that surrounds one and of which one cannot come out. One goes from one to the other as a prisoner and these exciting ideas are high, bristling with difficulties and their presence causes pain that one cannot get rid of. The waking in the middle of the night contains a decrease of consciousness. It welcomes the concern and it refuses to see its end. It is somewhat similar to the state in which one finds oneself after death, when remorse assails the soul which only has to defend itself, the light vision of reason. In both states one has lost the concept of the importance of things, and the ability to compare their reports of magnitude. But one of these states ends with the night, with the curtains drawn, the appearance of the morning. The other may have a much longer duration.

The one who sees in the succession of causes and effects, destroys the remorse of all actions by the understanding of these actions and of their legitimate place in the chain of life. He destroys the monster by penetrating its nature. He can also destroy it by the clear gaze of the wise indifference and dissolve it in front of him as an empty smoke.

When the fight against the monster is over, because everything ends by the consumption of time, the man must cross the bridge. He crosses it by virtue of its lightness.

The judgment that he has pronounced once, was not the number of his weight. The bridge is what separates the spiritual region from the temporary region, also called astral, where turn in a circular form, the terrestrial currents.

The man can only escape to these currents if his own density allows him to. To enter in the intelligible world, the thought has to form the matter of his new body.

A camel cannot pass through the whole of a needle. The man will only be able to enter the spiritual world if he has prepared in his life, a body, likely to support the rate of vibrations. When his instinctive forces will have died by exhaustion, according to his intelligence and his love, he will be left with an aerial envelop in which he will be easily able to cross the symbolic bridge. But if he does not have this envelop, if he is dominated by the desire to realize himself in flesh, he goes where his vision calls him, according to the forces which attracts him. Beside, the spiritual life does not tempt him. He does not aspire to live there. He is carried away by a confused enjoyment, by the circles of the earth. He feels the presence of the matter as a vivifying warmth. With all his ardor, he aspires to the seed of incarnation.

The significance of the last thought

— Never give up joy, said the Buddha to his son.

Joy is the secret of the world. In life, the strongest man is the happiest man. It is the same after death. The happy deceased faces without fear the ordeal of the scale, the one of the monster and that of the bridge. Joy is a fire of the soul on which one has to watch during his life, and one has to supply with brushwood of joyful thoughts. At the time of death, it is a load that has to be thrown on that fire for its brightness to illuminate the darkness in which one rushes.

The last thought has a great significance. It subsists in the sleep that follows the moment of death. Similar to an igneous arrow, which leads and allows to see the purpose.

When the man feels death coming, he must abolish the regret of the world of forms he abandons, he must concentrate on the wisdom of which he had made provision, gather in a bundle the branches of his knowledge and light them with his joy. He must be joyful of his new transformation and smile to what he will not see anymore. He must say to himself: The loved ones are not lost for me. I will still be united to them in reality, thanks to their love.

I will find them again under their familiar appearances, thanks to the strength of my memory. I will drag them with me by spiritualizing them, if they are less advanced than I am in the walk towards the mind. I will follow them with loyalty, and they will drag me, if by the grace of their effort, they precede me.

The man who feels death coming has to anticipate on the sleep which will follow it and make himself, mindfully, the ceremony of his judgment. He must, since the minute he was born, make the summary of his life, call, out of the shadow where they rest, all the accomplished actions, all the actions he has judged god or bad, according to his arbitrary design of good and evil. He must show the forty-two essential sins at the same time as the forty-two judges. And when they are grouped around him, he must gather all his will, all his evocative power and all his joy to accomplish the act of superior magic which is in the same time a cosmic sleight of hand.

He will cease the neck one of the forty-two bad actions, the greatest one if possible, the smallest one if the greatest one has a too terrible face for his courage, he will turn it around, will examine it in every angle and will discover the root which created it. He will date back to its cause and he will search for the cause of this cause. And in the measure of his imagination, he will go as far as he can in this research of causes. This will lead him to the origin of its life, to the origin of the life of his father and then to the one of the root. He will date back to the birth of the man, to the first movement of life on earth, to the creation of the solar system. He will go even further if he can, and he will see at the origin of all, a divine responsibility. And when he will have embraced the conceptions of solar systems through the miracle of infinites, he will consider the smallness of his bad action and its little importance in the general economy. And he will feel an unknown joy from it. He will laugh of the little importance of his bad action. He will consider it in all its insignificance. And the other forty-one bad actions will become worthless, will shrink until ceasing to exist, and the judges who only had a reality through them, will instantly fall into dissolution.

Thus the man, before dying, when he still enjoys of his mindfulness, must evoke what will happen to him after death, when his consciousness will be refused, that the privation of the body and the ignorance of the place he is will make him passive and amazed. He must predict the judgment, the scale and the arrival of the monster. He must judge and absolve himself in virtue of his puny character and of the weight of the immensity on the nothing he represents regarding them. And he must do it in joy.

Without doubt, he will find himself in very different conditions, at the time of the real judgment, when he will wake up from his posthumous sleep, before the panorama of his life. He will then be in an emotional element, which is opposite to the physical world, where the separateness is less, and where he will conceive the objects and creatures, as barely separated from him. The memory of an act of destruction made during his life, against a plant, an animal or a man, will appear to him as being practiced against himself. And it is this extension of egoism that facilitates the arise of remorse and gives them a devouring strength.

But if he has spoofed in his lifetime the formidable ceremony, if he covered it with the color of joy, he partly removed its suffering power. When it appears again, even if the deceased has only an uncertain consciousness, it has lost its seriousness and its importance. The joy with which one has created it at the first time, still envelops it. Because this kind of painting whose gaiety recovers the things is of a quality that has difficulty to fade and that the memory puts together.

The joy, the imponderable joy, is of cosmic essence. Where joy is, the remorse cannot push the smallest root. But it does not open the door of the spiritual world. It only gives momentum. It binds itself as well as to the material desire than to the spiritual one. With it, the one who is strongly attached to physical forms, will roll voluptuously in the round of the earth, towards the enjoyment given by the generation.

Joy needs to be purified. As wines which give different intoxications in virtue of the aristocracy of their aroma and the suns which have matured their vintages, there are higher joys than the last. In all is found a kind of common essence. But one has to, with a scholarly method, distinguish the joy of the earth from the one which favors the access to the world of the gods.

It is by an addition of the being and an affinity of its inner substance that the man can cross the bridge which leads to the spiritual life. At most, at the time of death, one will be able to support this transition by wrapping a lightweight garment of pure ideas. At that moment, the normal abilities are weakened, when reason falters, it is the dominant thought of life which takes over and it is on its wings that one is carried away.

The man must remember then what was his highest ideal and imagine it with all the strength he has left. As death can occur suddenly, he is exposed not having the necessary awareness. As a warrior who has no time to put on an armor at the time of the fight, he may not be able to collect the sparkling ideas that would have defended him. He must have trained for long to summarize his ideas in a symbolic image, in a divine face, in a geometric sign of an almost mechanical way, he will see hasten by the first call of thought. It is bad that this image represents a physical pain, a representation of torture. If it is a cross, it should be stripped of its body of crucified Christ, it should be a simple and pure cross as the spirit it has represented, from the earliest times. The symbol can be a shining face of Venus Aphrodite with her sea wave colored eyes, her crown of flowered roses and her spring hair. It may have the oval face that one has loved and that has reflected for one all the beauty of the earth. To be strictly practical, it would be better if the sign reminded the absolution given to oneself, the baptismal forgiveness of the spirit. But whatever it is, it must be colored by the joy of transformation, the joy of the new world, in which one will enter.

Symbolic geometry, design traced by the wisdom of all life, human face charged of reflections, divine face in the shape of a shield, it is behind it that the soul must come out of the corpse of the flesh, and under its protection must rush forward.

The meaning of incarnation

The egalitarian justice of which the man dreams does not exist.

After death, the posthumous law is exerted with the same transcendent absence of pity than during life, but it is exerted backwards. There are always stupid and egoist ones, intelligent and affectionate ones, but the possibilities of happiness are for those, and in a certain measure, the first ones are the last ones. The differences caused by wealth and poverty does not exist anymore and if sexual appetites remain, the body by which one is donned, wears no longer the sex mark. But the transformation is the vital law, the most striking phenomenon.

The beings are transformed with even more speed as they become less material. The more one descends towards the matter and the more there is solidity and lack of change. It is because of this ease of transformation that I said that the deceased where more unfaithful than the living. Furthermore, this transformation becomes an endless source of enjoyment, but this enjoyment is only visible at a certain degree of development. It is the sign of mediocrity wanting to remain endlessly similar to oneself. The more the transformation is rapid the more there is communion with nature, participation to the laws of life. But, naturally, it is necessary in order to feel this enjoyment, of which we have no idea on earth, to have stripped a part of our own egoism and the love we feel for our hard envelop.

The vital difference of the beings after death is in their will of direction. Most, almost all, are moved by a blind desire to lock themselves in a new terrestrial form. They are called towards the world of the physical condensation. They want to be composed again by elements of slow changing, by the liquids of the blood, the atoms of the flesh, the mineral of bones. A very small number, those who could store the sense of the world in the profoundness of their being, aspire to be saved from the physical matter and vibrate in unison of the mind. These two categories of beings meet and move along, each towards different destinies. The great, the unique separation of those who love each other is not achieved by the ordinary death of which we know the sadness. It takes place at the time of the decision which launches one towards the world of the mind and the other to the one of earth. And it is then irrevocable. Thus those who love each other have to watch carefully, for too great changes not to happen in nature while one is alive and the other dead, but also to have a spiritual development roughly the same to avoid the definitive separation which reincarnates one and which allows the other to escape the earth.

After the panorama of the last life has uncoiled in front of him, then, the man chooses. He chooses in virtue of the love determined in its substance. Almost always, the choice throws him towards what he has loved, towards the pleasures he is used to and as for feeling the pleasures, physical organs are needed, he aspires to possess these organs.

What longing he feels then! What uncontrollable thrust, painful as a burn! He ceases to see the forms, he only perceives their silent double, the mysterious figure of their essence. He let himself go in a semiconscious dizziness, of circular currents as the planet; which arise from it and turn in its movement. According to its attractions, the man will preferably go towards the places where he has enjoyed physically. He answers to calls, all the links created once by him attracts him, he rolls, here and there, driven by the temptations that its desires give rise to. The one who has loved forests is attracted by the magnetism released by the trees. The one who has lived on water, floats on the mists of the sea, goes up and down with the foam, swoons one the sand of the shores. The cities with their gatherings of humans have formidable charms. The beings who wander in the invisible currents see the chimneys as spectral signs indicating that under the cover of the roofs there are carnal heat of bodies, presences whose reconciliation procures pleasure. The bell towers of churches are not images of prayers for them, but ghosts who testify in the space beneath them that men are gathered for the collective enjoyment.

They mingle with all that is life, they swirl in denser troops into the crowds, they land, such as flies, wherever there is a little blood. For blood, animal or human blood, the prepared matter for life has a receiving power of the creature that aspires to live, and gives it a confused satisfaction, a foretaste of what it wants.

But it is the attractive seed. It is the sexual smell, the generative wet seed, especially the one of the ma, which contains the most powerful power of appeal.

Similarly, as there are animals who go towards a water puddle across immense deserts, as there are birds of prey who have knowledge of a carrion lying in a huge distance, thus the beings of the afterlife go to the seed intended for them. They find it in virtue of their own affinities. Each fellow goes towards his fellow. There is a sense of direction that one might call the meaning of the incarnation. The man finds his group again and in his group he finds again those he has loved and hated in previous lives. It is by this group that is produced the seed in which there will be the best development facilities, the greatest power of enjoyment. It is in this group that the seed will fall into the most maternal matrix, the matrix where for nine months, he will prepare in damp darkness to see again the light of the lost sun.

He will prepare himself by shaping with substance of the mother's body, the new envelop by which will be satisfied the imperious desires that pushes him. He will work its best, carving his head with his own thought, shaping its for, according to the use he wants to made of it and according to the materials, good or bad, which he has at his disposal. The collaborator towards whom he ran, because she called him, will help him with the juices of her flesh and the fluids of her essence. He will prepare physical disabilities, resulting from his negligence of weaving and carving, the absences of moral qualities, results of his ignorance. He will put nine months to complete this imperfect work.

But the birth in the best seed has its challenges. One must find this best seed. To find it, one must answer a call, be attracted by the creators. The more one is loved, the more one is called. Woe then to the egoist who made himself voluntarily lonely! ... Woe to he who left within him to obscure the meaning of the incarnation. He may not hear the appeal. And it may be that no one calls while the one who has loved a lot and was loved a lot will have the choice in the attractions. Anyhow, there is a period of research, of waiting, which is only semiconscious.

There are blind and deaf deceased; clairvoyant deceased and with delicate hearing. There are especially deceased in whom the desire of the matter is great. The death whose nature is rude, the dead who let himself dominate by a physical passion, may divert from his path and rush in any lower seed where he will be able to satisfy more rapidly this passion.

It is wise to develop, in the measure when it is possible, during one's life, the meaning of incarnation. The one who has within him more love is the one who incarnates more easily. We will see that this wealth of love is also a condition to escape to incarnation. The ability of love and the sum of wisdom establish the hierarchy of the beings. The last ones on earth become the first ones if they are rich in intelligence and love.

The last ones on earth stay the last ones, if they are ignorant and selfish. But in reality, there are neither first nor last ones. There are blind and careless ones on one hand, and on the other hand there are beings who are aware and who enjoy the comprehension of things. The emotional is where communication from one to the other is easier than in the physical world and where only his expansion procures him joy. The intelligent who draws all joy from the intelligence glimpses an endless field for the game of his thought. And the one and the other, thanks to their qualities, are pushed towards the seed of their race, and of their group, where they will be incarnated in better conditions, if one's judges, yet that there might be good conditions to enter in the captivity of planet earth.

The threat of animalism

Men in their pride have always revolted to the idea that a man, with his sublime faculties could reincarnate even accidentally, in an animal body. Modern philosophers — those who believe in reincarnation — to satisfy this , have decreed that there was between the reigns an absolute separation. They called rude superstition a belief that was shared by the Buddha, by Pythagoras, Plato and Plotinus, that is to say the highest minds of humanity.

There is possibility of incarnation in an animal body when the sum of desires in human consciousness rather corresponds to the desires of an animal consciousness than a human consciousness. There are no watertight compartments between the changing forms of life and each takes the form that corresponds best to the addition of his actions and thoughts in a trend. A trend of ferocity is better expressed in a ferocious animal, an immoderate taste of race in some small animal that spends its time running. There are men who have no sublime faculty, who even have no desire to use their faculty of thinking. Endeavor in the field of thought, represents even for some a horrible possibility . Purely affective tendencies, pushed to the extreme, such as loyalty, will be realized better, for example in a dog than a man.

An unsatisfied passion can exceptionally demote the man into the animal, by hastiness of satisfaction. The fall is then deeper than usual back in the human kingdom to which condemn themselves, with ineffable joy of life, the vast majority of men. The Buddha has taught that one may even fall from a greater height. Desire is sovereign. Even when one has surpassed the human stage and has reached the one of gods the call of desire, its immediate needs to be satisfied, brings in some cases, the animal kingdom. And that is why he preached no other wisdom, as sovereign key of the world, than the total destruction of desire.

Every man, even reaching a certain degree of wisdom, has experienced

this tyrannical character of desire who wants to be satisfied in an immediate way. What sacrifices we accomplish in life to a realization obtained
on the spot! The attraction of the body is a compelling power. Driven by
this attraction, a coarse soul which did not give life to its intelligence,
which only has physical instincts to achieve, sometimes rushes into a
beast seed where growth is faster and where, therefore, the instincts are
satisfied sooner. It is however an exception.

If we focus with a greater concern for brotherhood, on animal species,
one would find there often the signs that resemble them to us. Some
clairvoyants or rather some clairaudient, claim to have heard from the
animals, calls, reproachful cries, uttered towards their forgetful brothers. Careful observation of animals allows to find in them movements
of intelligence that go beyond the capacity of their organs, beyond the
capabilities of their reign. It is mostly among wild animals that exist
faculties which, to some extent, are human.

Moreover, there is not movement that generates its opposite. If there
is an urge toward the spiritual, there is a flashback, an urge towards the
material. There is no man who has not felt within himself, at certain
times, this retrograde momentum. The animal aspiration is hidden
within us and wakes up with the suggestion of some desires. Under
the influence of hunger, the man is totally dominated by an instinct of
food absorption. The sexual appetite changes it, even if he has reached
a certain degree of reason in an animal only eager to show its male or
female quality.

Animal imitation plays a great role in the lives of men and the most
cultivated devote themselves, not without pride. Sport, which has taken
such an important place in our Western societies, is only a form of this
imitation. Animal models are by the bye never met. No runner crosses
distances with the speed of the horse. What are the best swimmers
alongside the fastest fish? On their imperfect devices, which airmen
could equal the birds?

The same applies for the generating effort. The man who has many
children, imitating the fertility of the animal, prints to his trends a retrograde movement because in the species scale, it is the most prolific

that are the most inferior. His merit is only a selfishness compounded of a desire for multiplicity.

The retrograde strength lies in us and we undergo it unwittingly. It pushes us to crawl, to quaff to drink, to climb trees to entertain us. But sometimes a man lets himself be dominated by an animal instinct. Under the color of pleasure that instinct takes the form of his ideal. If this man, by the fact of his bad luck, dies at the time of the satisfaction of his instinct, when all his forces are focused to achieve it, he will carry this ideal through death as its only conductive lamp. At the time of his new incarnation, this blind will be attracted, despite himself, to the creature whose organs will be able to carry to their maximum, the qualities he has desired. With delight, he will seize a beast seed where will easily express the animal ideal of his human life.

But this fall is rare and cannot be long-term. What is one life in all the lives in which every creature has to go? The being who has been human will be called urgently by what he has lost. He is accustomed to the expression by the word. It is the desire to speak by root words that will become within him the predominant desire, haunting and, which will bring him back in a man's body. The desperate fixity with which some animals are watching us when we speak, is only the nostalgia of the lost verb. For the desire that precipitates the fall is also the instrument of salvation. The laws of nature, always have two sides. By desire one descends. By desire one go back up and it is the quality of the desire that makes one go up or down.

***

How will I find the true measure in the complication of laws? How wouldn't I lose myself in the mysterious labyrinth of the future? Especially how to escape to that threat of animalism? Since it is true that everyone weaves its physical fibers, prepares the quality of his blood and the solidity of his bones in the maternal womb, it must be true that the shape of each man keeps a certain resemblance to the form of his previous life. The similarity of the creator must generate the similarity of the mold.

Thus I saw with certainty the memory of animal lives registered on many faces around me. I remember a charming friend who looked so much like a dumbfounded nestling that I was instinctively looking with my hand the velvety of feathers along its body. Another one had kept from the family of peacocks which she came from, the ostentatious habit to display her beauty to seduce the richness of the gift. How many fearful characters have received their fear and their sheep-like faculty of imitation of the species of sheep! How many have in the shape of their head, the aspect of a wolf, pork or fox! Of an old cock life, haven't some of them kept an outrageous taste of polygamy, a pretentious need of female domination. On some, the aquatic element exerts an irresistible attraction and others, when they see trees, immediately feel the desire to go up there.

I feel within me shake all animal instincts and I am afraid that one of them, by the power of some recollection, will tyrannically seize me. Sometimes I feel, not as hope but as a reminiscence, the delight to crawl under the scales reflected by the snake, to lock myself in a rolling house, modelled on the tortoise. I galloped freely on moors with wild horses. I washed myself on manures with joy to soil my hair, when I belonged to a family of wild boars. As a sad dog, I barked at the moon in autumn nights. As a lark deprived of reason, I got up in the first hour of the day to count the drops of dew which moistened my beak. In barnyards, I aspired to freedom. Free, I looked with admiration, from the edge of woods, the mysterious figure of men. I dug up the dead when I was jackal, I was aristocrat when I was a giraffe, I spent entire lives making jokes when I was a monkey. I received arrows, I fell into traps, my herd abandoned me when I was injured. I was hungry, I was thirsty. My main concerns have been food research, female pursuit. My greatest joys have been the heat of nest or den, beak caresses, muzzle proximities. And I was always afraid of my ugliness when I saw my reflection in the water.

My God! How all these lives were similar to the human life! My God! How the degree I have stepped is minimal and how would I be foolish to boast about it! My God! Keep me free from the animalism that I bear within me!

The possibility to choose one's next incarnation

It is by a strange mystery, mystery that touches the one of justice and injustice, that men incarnate in a body rather than in another one. It is more enjoyable to be attractive than ugly. It seems more convenient to develop in a rich environment rather than a poor one. If one enjoyed of the faculty of choice, almost every man would be born attractive and rich. In what measure one has this precious faculty to choose and what are the laws that conduct the currents of the shape being formed?

It is on these laws that nature has thrown its most hermetic veil. They are so complex that it is difficult to recognize oneself in their intersections. However, it appears that if there is, to some extent, a faculty of happy choice, it belongs to the most intelligent and those who have cultivated a love power.

The man creates constantly causes and effects. Except that he does not always recognize the effects he has created. The surprise that some effects provide him comes from the oversight by which his soul is covered at the time of his fall in the birth. But even if this beneficent oversight only freed him temporarily from his poor obsessions, his hatred and his loves, he would not understand the complicated fabric of causes and effects. Much of the pain that strike us are created by our own foolishness, during our youth. This does not prevent us from cursing the fate that has nothing to do with it. One cause often produces its effects before our eyes, in a few years, without us being able to discern anything. Discernment is sometimes impossible because there are effects that extend from one life to another and causes that seem to have no effect, because without our input, by an inner reaction, we have annihilated these effects. What the philosophy of India calls Karma is less rigorous than we said. Our Karma is exercised within ourselves, in our tendencies, and we are therefore likely to modify and sometimes destroy it. Repentance is an indirect form of the annihilation of Karma. It is slower than if it was direct, that is to say conscious.

The world of the physical life is the one where we mainly produce lower causes, physical causes that have effects of the same nature. The world in which we live in after death is the one of higher causes. There is no possibility of creating causes in the spirit world for those who have attained a certain development and regained full conscious-ness.

The ordinary law, the one that plays for the majority, makes the man incarnate in a man's seed. But how is it then that we suffer the defects and diseases of his parents or that we benefit from their qualities? Why by being born one is lame, why the other has the advantage of long hair and a slender waist?

We incarnate in swarms. Like bees, human beings form swarms. The apparent chances of life are produced by the instinctive movements of the units of the swarm that tend to meet for exchange of good and evil. We are linked to a small group of the swarm. We are to a certain extent part of the close relatives that we loved and that attracts you. If they have faculties, tastes, diseases, they owe them very often to you, to your actions and your thoughts in previous lives. They only give you back, when you enter the physical seed, what you have given them. Let's take the example of a serious illness, the tuberculosis. The being by incarnating, finds it in the materials of which his body is composed. But there is only one exchange. He has given, he receives in turn. If he nurtured within him a desire strong enough of health, he will keep the potential disease in his seed, he will prevent it from manifesting through his taste for health. He will neutralize through this effort his physical Karma.

Often there is no manifestation of heredity. It means that the being incarnated among strangers. Having only little in common with his parents, he has the opportunity, while working on his body in the maternal womb, to repel disease's seeds that are foreign to him and with which he has no affinity. But he will benefit hardly for the same reason of the contribution of hereditary qualities.

The one who desired with ardor in previous lives the beauty of the face and the form, will implement this desire and has many chances to sculpt himself attractive. His lower passions, even if they are numerous and horrible, will try in vain to counteract him and to print on his features. The desire has a powerful force. This is why we see creatures full of physical perfection that has no correlation with the imperfection of their soul. Our past actions have indirect repercussions on the creation of our new form at the time of the incarnation.

This backlash is exercised by ourselves. If, for example, I consciously make someone a physical injury, I hold to an intelligible principle of form that has its reflection within me and my creative quality is diminished.

Plato thought that there were eternal essences, spiritual principles, to the contemplation from which attained the superior man after his death and sometimes during his lifetime. An action of violence we commit, corresponds in ourselves to a deformation of a spiritual principle. This deformation will occur at the time of the incarnation, through an inability to build a beautiful shape. The one who upsets in him the genius of the form, remains a mediocre creator. Thus, to some extent, manifests a certain justice, according to our design.

Except that this justice is slow and it has neither the appearance nor the qualities we ideally attribute to an immanent justice. It does not strike the guilty from the outside, but it springs from within his heart, by modifying its capabilities. What we call remorse and what can be considered as a form of punishment, creates in the soul, by its dark and dreadful work, the opposite qualities of the action we regret having done.

The being transformed by remorse feels new affinities and is attracted, at the time of the incarnation, by a new environment, under these affinities. But no matter how high and noble the affinities are, no matter how perfect is the environment in which one is called by its history, the one who has in him a strong desire to live can still rush blindly towards the coarsest environment of its swarm, for an immediate realization. Thus the hungry traveler in search of food, regardless of his wealth, will sit down to table in the inn of beggars and be satisfied with a rough wine and an onion with his bread.

If one considers that the main goal is to find those we love and to be born in an environment where the spirit will not be oppressed, care must be taken not to have in oneself this devouring hunger. The hunger for physical pleasure which is the lot of almost all men is a greater danger, to obtain a favorable incarnation, that all the consequences of actions that we usually call bad. The most frightening aspect of evil in the afterlife is the immoderate taste of physical life which veils the meaning of the incarnation and prevents to choose well his fathers.

The meaning of the incarnation can also be veiled by our desire to find someone we loved and who placed himself before us, in a lower environment where evil dominates. In our effort to follow him, we risk to opt for seeds responsible for defects that we do not deserve and whose weight will be a source of pain.

Thus we will do the cruellest experiments of all. What we felt to be the best, the affection for a fraternal creature, will make us downgrade instead of raising us. We will give him a proof of love he will always ignore and that we ourselves ignore, while we will be enlightened in this form by the sun of the earth. But the wheel of fortune turns incessantly. Lives succeed, numerous and different, and no matter how imperfect the creatures fed by the grain of misfortune are, they always take a small advantage of having been creature.

The absolution of the Catholic religion after confession is a wise mean to allow men to die and wake up after death in a desirable peace with themselves. This peace has influence on the meaning of the incarnation. But the absolution given by a priest, would he be a pope, works only on average souls. These ones, passing through intermediate currents in a state of semi-consciousness, content themselves with this vague satisfaction of themselves that they have received with the magical sign of the priest.

But the elevated souls, when they recover their full consciousness, are forced to revise the absolution given by man in the name of God. They know that there is only judgment in front of his own court, absolution than one gave to oneself and that the divine wisdom is shaped such that it produces only illusory pardons pending the only true forgiveness which is begotten by the spirit and gushes like a flower springs from a shrub.

One should not have a too severe soul, in order not to judge too wrongly. On the shrub that should give the flower, one must not pour corrosive substances. Scruples that eat up, the prejudices that destroy, persist after death and thwart greatly the forgiveness which is so essential to agree to oneself.

Happy is he who by a liberal vision of things, through a harmonious emancipation of human barriers, attains the knowledge of the highest causes, knowledge by which the human sin becomes worthless! Happy is he who joyfully absolves himself and who in the lightness of his forgiveness, sails towards the most favorable incarnation!

Ways to discern one's past incarnations

Many people think that since they do not recall their past lives, it means that these lives have never occurred. Others believe in their existence, but bitterly regret not having preserved its memory. Yet the so ruthless law of nature had no other precious favor for the man than forgetting the past. When souls enter the prison of the living flesh, they drink the divine water of the river that the ancients called Lethe and of which, more educated than us, they recognized the benefit.

At the degree of our development, still dominated as we are by the principle of hatred, we would only dream to meet our grudges, wreak vengeance. We would not consider the change suffered by the creatures between two lives and the change we experienced ourselves. The experience that the view of old mistakes would give us, would be sadly compensated by the greatest mistakes that this knowledge would make us commit.

As the spirit rises in the hierarchy of the spirit, it conquers a greater possibility to see his past unfold before his eyes. Everyone has the memory that he deserves or rather he can withstand. A time still very far will come, when the man will have the privilege to find back in his consciousness, the memory of all his lives. But perhaps will he use this privilege only with great caution. He will understand what hidden delight contained the waters of Lethe and the sweetness of not knowing.

Moreover, under the thick veil that covers our thinking, we have some capabilities to see emerge in the mist, the ghosts of our past lives.

The safest indication is the one that comes from our instinctive impulses, obscure tendencies that push us towards certain people rather than others. It is wise to carefully consider these indications because our whole existence is subject to the meeting of a small number of individuals who must play a role in our life, either to help or to delay it, either to make us happy, or to make us suffer.

I often regretted not being a scholar versed in the knowledge of mechanical laws, along with the subtle science of waves and currents. I would have tried to invent a device that would have been more useful than the automobile engine or the telephone. This device, which delicacy would have been extreme, would have allowed the man to know where in the world is the being of opposite sex, with whom he has affinities and is likely to make the exchange of love. This device would have included a world map with a point or points that would have enlightened to indicate the places he should go in order to make the desired meeting. Perhaps inventors have thought like me, about the invention of this engine, indicative of sympathy and they were arrested by the difficulties of fulfillment.

We can attain through careful observation to a useful knowledge of the game of affinities.

Everyone can see that in the first years of his youth, one discovers with enough speed all the characters, good or bad, that will play a role in your life. It seems that fate has wanted everyone to do a sort of summary of all the wonders of affection that the human swarm has for him in which he placed himself, more or less consciously. All these characters discovered in the first rush to know life, are the ancient relations of the previous existence. One creates naturally new bonds, but the most important are mysteriously gathered in early youth. The new relationships made in middle age for example, can also, but only as an exception, be relations of the past life.

By making a connection between the essential trends of the different individuals who play a role in your life and seem to have been in your previous life, have the notion of a particular group. It is then necessary to attempt to link this group to the being that we are ourselves. With the help of a reminiscence, of the particular taste one has for a time, or of the reminiscence and the taste that can the individuals in the group reveal, it happens that one clarifies the time and place where this swarm incarnated previously. By reconstitutions, by analyzing trends in sloughed characters one can go further, until the discovery of some past love or hate states. But imagination and poetic fantasy are likely to play a great role in this kind of research.

The prolonged introspection methods only give poor results. One could go further by causing states of somnambulism. A. de Rochas recorded his experiences in a large volume that is quite convincing. It shows topics downgrade in time under the influence of the magnetic sleep. They stammer and speak baby talk, when they get to their first childhood, they withdraw into themselves, the arms to the body and the fists in the eyes, when they are supposed to be in the days when they lived in the belly of their mother. The physiognomy is always linked to the personality through which they pass and the painful or joyful minute they describe. The subject makes plausible stories and traces of characters whose lives we could sometimes verify the existence. Unfortunately, these stories, which sometimes affect history, contain improbabilities and anachronisms. Their mass and consistency are nevertheless impressive. But one should not know himself mediums who are usually used in this kind of experience. It may be that I always came at a bad time. But those in whose presence I was, emanated as a tangible atmosphere, a conscious and organized lie. Few passes of a sincere hypnotist were sufficient so that they were projected with ease, with too much ease, through a distant life and always illustrious. No, no, said then within me an inner voice that never betrays me. Most mediums conform their visions to a spiritualist religion of which they have ordinarily knowledge. They obey its narrow and strict morality and they ensure to confirm the punishment of its hell and the childish joys of its paradise.

However, there is in the book of A. de Rochas several statements that should be noted, coming from topics that seem most truthful. Several noted that while incarnating, they were dragged, despite themselves, by the current of the irresistible force. From this follows, besides the latent desire of life, a cosmic law would precipitate in the form creatures and that those who want to escape this form would have to implement a more powerful force, issued from their will.

A subject of poor development, sleepwalking, following the course of his lives and reaching the fourth declared, with some shame, that it was a monkey life and that he had kept from it the animal passions.

A. de Rochas did not took the matter seriously and would have a hard time not laughing. Such a statement nevertheless contained no pleasant character and should have been for him, a subject of meditation.

This series of experiments is still very interesting by the indication it gives on the delay separating the lives between them. Plato had set, in general, this period to a thousand years. But maybe he thought of the lives of philosophers, the only men who had an interest in his eyes, and in the eyes of the wise who have scrutinized these problems in Antiquity. The Stoic Chrysippus thought that only philosophers have an existence after death. Modern theosophists who have produced an abundant literature about the afterlife have postponed this period, to an average intelligence, of fifteen hundred years. It is true that they returned to this opinion and have diminished the time so imprudently set.

The experiments of A. de Rochas show that the general law of the succession of lives wants that one passes from one to the other, almost without intervals. All his subjects are people barely educated, often even coarse. The proof is that they are unanimous in describing a period of darkness after death and a confused struggle to conquer clarity.

The elapsed period between two incarnations is infinitely variable and it is this variation that has created so many diverse opinions. As in the terrestrial life, some die after one day because they do not have an organism strong enough and others at ninety years, by virtue of their strength, as, in life after death, those who only have a miserable spiritual body are sucked immediately through the incarnation and those who have a viable spiritual body spend long years before incarnating.

The law is strictly the same as on earth. The rich man, among the living greedy of speculation and wealth, is the one who has the best chance to get richer, because he possesses the necessary instrument. In the afterlife the intelligent man is the one who has the best chance to become more intelligent, that is to say, to have a happy lot. The possession of faculty allows the development of the faculty. This, in our language, can be called justice as well as injustice. It is better to call it law.

The time that separates the lives depends less on the development of each individual than his desire to return to the form. If we take a man gathering the greatest possible amount of intellectuality, the length of time he will live between two lives will depend on the physical desires that he had felt in the last years of his life. If he has issued a sincere and strong desire not to return to earth, this desire joined to the extent of his intelligence, will suffice to keep him from reincarnating, at least for an incalculable period of years. And as the faculty of change is all the greater than the thought is active, when he will reappear on earth, his trends will be changed so much that no one will be able to make an approximation with his former personality. If, however, by growing older, he had close affections, these ones will call him back with his group, and will call him back all the more powerfully that he will be linked to this group. An ordinary man, without intellectual development, does not change between two lives and returns, somewhat similar to himself.

It is a fact recognized by those who have studied the laws of reincarnation that this ordinary man brings by giving birth to the overall physical characteristic of his last existence. Each built in the maternal womb the human type he knows best, and which is the type of his last existence. One sees sometimes born in France, of French parents, a child having for example a Hindu or Chinese type. In vain, one looked in the past for the approximation of a Hindu or Chinese with their foremothers. In these cases, one always recognizes that the child is out of place in the society where he is. To succeed he has not the same practical qualities than others. In general, Hindus reincarnate among Hindus, French among the French. The attraction even calls the beings in the same families. But there are a large number of exceptions. As if they aspired to the variety of new lands, the souls migrate. These migrations have forerunners and latecomers. Both the are isolated among unknown groups.

The information that one can obtain from right and left, among particularly sensitive people have a strangely disappointing nature. I cannot explain to myself the great role played by Mary Stuart on the imagination of women. I have carefully read the history of this queen, I knew so little about and my curiosity was not satisfied. A very large number of women were Mary Stuart in a past life and after her Cleopatra is one that meets most votes. When it comes to past incarnations each and even among the most reasonable, choose in the history, famous people, one would have wanted to be. Oh extraordinary prestige of royalty for childish souls! Some, less foolish, opt for those that have distinguished themselves by thinking rather than power. Students of theosophy have lost a lot of time with these childish games and their leaders gave them the example of royal incarnations. Some modest, contempt themselves to have been the followers of the masters. Modesty mixed with pride has recently has recently allowed a young woman to find within herself the personality of Judas Iscariot and has sincerely made the confession of the thirty denarius received.

The dream, in this kind of research can sometimes combine with some reality. But it is almost always illusionary when it is based on the choice of sympathy or that of admiration*. This illusion has been that of many people, overcome by the vanity to remember and which compensates for the occult knowledge by imagination.

---

* Mr. Bozzano in several of his interesting works has given examples of recollections of past lives and has provided in the same time, the most convincing evidence. There are also indisputable cases in Mr. G. DELANNE's book, *Les preuves de la réincarnation.*

Ways to discern one's last incarnation by the contour of the shadow

We can see a vague and general indication on the time and the country where our past life went by, by a method which is personal to me and that I deliver because I sincerely believe that it corresponds to a reality. It is of easy application, and each will be able to easily try to put it into practice.

I had always been very struck in my childhood by the great difference which exists between our shadow and the silhouette of ourselves that we get to know by looking at us in a mirror. Childhood is the only period in life where one has the power and the audacity to wonder. Many of these surprises and the explanation given to them as a child deserve to be collected and used.

I happened very often in the early years of my life not to recognize myself in my shadow and turn around to see if it was not produced by another person than me. I marveled at the oddness of this dark twin and I found it so foreign to myself that I expected at every moment to see him detach and get away under an autonomous will.

I only accustomed myself after many years to its changing fantasy.

Many people have recognized that something mysterious, having an intimate relationship with our life and death, was hiding in our shadow. A. de Pouvourville recounted a strange way of bewitchment in use in Indochina. The sorcerer who wants someone's death must surprise him in the sun, a day when his shadow is stretching behind him with a particular clarity. So he looks at him square in the face and with a lance he took in this view, he lanced his shadow instead of the heart. From that moment, he is in possession of his life. When the sorcerer launches the lance from the earth, the man dies.

In a Tibetan book entitled: "The mirror that shows death" is indicated a method to know the approximate time of one's end, by mean of his shadow*.

On a clear day, one has to stand, legs apart, a stick in one's hand and watch its shadow carefully. When the attention is extreme, one can distinguish, or rather one must distinguish in the shadows, a white glow that fades. Immediately one must lift his eyes and one sees then cut in the sky, as in a mirror, the contour of his figure. If this vision is very clear, it is the sign that one has many days to live. If it is veiled, it means that life will be short and that one only enjoys a weak health. If the sky reflects no image, it means that death is coming.

I have experienced with all the sincerity and attention required. My shadow has remained a uniform color without white mixture. No doubt that what the Tibetans call attention, demands fixity which my mind is incapable of. I renounced to see my shadow in the blue sky, but I do not judge, as so many people, that an experience is impossible because I cannot manage to fulfill it.

I think there in the dark, as absurd as it may seem, a priori, an essence of us impossible to analyze. This essence has to do with our past. The shadow faithfully keeps a certain picture of that past. It is by meditating on the past lives in which I lived, that I managed to understand their relationship with the shadow that I drag behind me as inevitable as my old souls.

The shadow looks like us sometimes, but not always. It expresses a different character, sometimes much more charming and friendly than the person we are, sometimes rude and cartoonish being that we would despise if we did not find a certain tie with ourselves. The shadow is all the more resembling that these are simple people who have not undergone any change from one life to the other and which the two lives were separated only by a very short period. A man who, by a sudden excess of development would have undergone a deep transformation from one life to another, would certainly have a shadow completely unrecognizable. This case is very rare, and, in general, a man looks like his shadow.

To discover some features of his previous life one must use his intuition, without allowing one naturally to surrender to the invention

* Mrs. David NEEL relates this method in *Initiations and Initiates in Tibet*.

and act with the help of this material fulcrum issued from oneself. This fulcrum which is the shadow of his silhouette, must be used by a clear moonlight night. The moonlight, more than the one of the sun, without me being able to discern why, makes the shade revealing. It seems to give it a faculty of becoming personal and to express the old fainted character. From what I was able to deduce, it is only the character of the last life that the shade reveals.

I am well aware that we can explain the variations of the shade by laws of reflection of light. But what we cannot explain is a mystery of the contour, the essence of another creature which, if it walks with you, and mimics your movements without forgetting one, seems however to have a different way of feeling.

This revealing stranger, this tireless double, sometimes shrinks to the point of becoming dwarf, sometimes stretches like a giant. Sometimes he seems to be animated by an unknown maliciousness, he is sometimes resigned, sometimes sad, a sadness beyond our everyday sadness. He does not content himself by expressing an inexplicable report what we were in a previous life, he expresses it with the general characteristic of the costume. The shadow of a naked man has less language than the shadow of a dressed man. The garment helps the revelation of the past personality, it reflects the lost passions, the exercises to which one delivered himself in a body that no longer exists.

If intuition plays an important role in this search for past life, it would be necessary to have a thorough knowledge of costumes and hairstyles worn by ancient peoples. Many aspects will remain inexplicable to those who will study them because of their ignorance of how they dressed in time or in the country where they previously lived. Because the shadow has the art of creating with almost anything the distinctive mark of a race and an epoch. But it is still necessary to recognize this distinctive mark when it is indicated.

During the studies of shadows that I recently indulged, I saw Greeks, Arabs, I saw warriors of the Middle Ages. While carefully considering my own shadow — it is always on oneself that the experiences are the easier — I had the satisfaction of discovering there no characteristic of lost kingship. My cane, instead of taking the appearance of a scepter, will always extend in a stick of obvious hardiness. My hat, instead of turning into miter or crown, became a pretty miserable bonnet. I was followed by Languedoc shepherd, a simple man whose appearance betrayed by whatever an aspiration for spirituality.

I thought I recognized, during this research, that members of a whole group united by ties of friendship have had one last life, spent in Cambodia. Their shadows were Cambodians shadows. A certain love of this country, a view of life quite opposite to that of the West and various aspects of their life, seemed to come to support this hypothesis. But it is a prodigiously unverifiable hypothesis.

The shadow of animals also reveals, in some cases, the memory of a species which is not theirs, but in which they were previously able to have their animal place. I saw a dog with a fox's shadow, and another with a buffalo's shadow. I thought that an effort towards intelligence could have determined among these dogs, once fox and once buffalo, a transmigration in a more developed species where their efforts had their realization.

Furthermore, it is given to each to make a more detailed study of this question and to become through long walks, with friends, in the moonlight, a master in interpretation and shadow science.

The spiritual world

As a vivid branch that spurts in spring of a tree and quickly gives solid sheets, thus grown within me with a mysterious greenness, the desire not to be reincarnated in the race of pain that grows and multiplies on earth. I consider the realization of this desire as possible, even if it is not certain. A constant desire, a careful application, or the science of some clever method discovered by a wise inventor, will get me to the result I want.

So that I leave my fellow men, that men's love fills my soul and that knowledge of things lights it!

All men do not reincarnate. Those who are well judged and who, after the solemn minute of the judgment have inflicted no punishment to themselves, those who, on the wings of their joy, have easily crossed the bridge that separates one world from the other, attain "the world of the sun" of the Hindus, the kingdom of the spirit, the Father's right. Blessed are those, and may I be among them as my hope promises me!

All those who have tried to describe the state in which one is in the spiritual world, agreed that it was an indescribable state by words and it was almost impossible to represent to oneself the joys and especially the activities. According to Plato, philosophers who have passed through purifications, that is to say those who, according to him, are at the top of the scale of beings, "live in houses that are not easy to describe." Socrates, in the Phaedo, speaks of a "pure residence", but about to describe it, he said, "in this case, he has not the required time."

It is a shame! Especially since he said this after a speech whose term has the value of a volume. And he adds — that is before drinking the hemlock that he speaks – "it is better for him to go take a bath, in order not to give women the trouble of washing a corpse."

It would have been better that women, whose job it was, have that inconvenience! We would have, according to this sage, the description of the world where he directly went after leaving the meeting of his followers. But perhaps he has meet the difficulty that all wise and all clairvoyants have encountered, when they wanted to talk about the spiritual life. Dante, after abundantly taking pleasure in describing the torments of hell, shows a strange poverty of knowledge at the time of giving views of the paradise.

Egyptians speak of singing, lectures and games. The Veda promises joy and the satisfaction of desires. In the Swarga, the highest subdivision of his heavenly stays under the chairmanship of Indra, we hear the Gandharvas, wonderful musicians, and we see the Apsaras dance, ideal dancers with a light body. Chinese Buddhists imagine rains of flowers, pavilions on the banks of rivers and macaws flights with beautiful wings. In the Fortunate isles of Hesiod, we pick fruits and one do not work. In the Champs Elysees of Pindar, the gymnasium exercises play a great role, in those of Virgil one plays lyre and love each other in delicious shades. The Koran promises young slaves and houris "with white skin like an ostrich egg"; Jesus promises a stay of happiness where one will especially enjoy the company of the patriarchs and prophets.

All these havens have as base the realization of human desires, the only ones which, according to the most elementary logic, cannot be realized there. They correspond to a craving for enjoyment which especially satisfies the instinct of laziness and a vague love of music and perfumes. But if these pleasures are not realized in a similar reality to ours, they are however to some extent and the promises of havens are not misleading. The man purified by the judgment that he has made on himself, is in a world where thought is creative. He creates what he imagines. He lives with his dreams which became real for him. He lives in pavilions along the river banks, he sees the Apsaras dance, and he enjoys the beauty of their dance. He engages himself in the exercises of the gymnasium, he walks under the delicious shades, he speaks for a long time with patriarchs and prophets.

But so long and pleasant as are the dreams, they end. It happens in life to imagine with all its details a desirable event. One starts again very often, accepting its fictional approval. But one does not start again eternally. There comes a time where our creative force is exhausted and where the pleasure we derive from it is dried up. In the spiritual world, as the creation is infinitely more real, the enjoyment is infinitely greater. There comes a time when it ceases. As in the physical life one is face to face with the surrounding reality. Thus ends the first part of human life in the spiritual world. All men do not live that first part of the dream. Some are unimaginative; others who voluntarily refuse to imagine, not having the taste of the lyre sounds and rains of flowers, nor even the one of talks with prominent figures. Their consciousness is awakened and they rush forward without respect and full of curiosity.

Swedenborg the clairvoyant ensures that when one enters the spiritual world, he is welcomed by angels and he distinguishes, according to a hierarchy, all kinds of angelic societies. This world, which is for him the heavenly stay of the Catholic God is the subtler reproduction of our universe, or rather our universe is only its deformation. The physical sun is like a dark nebula and the moon seems to be a moon spectrum.

For Swedenborg, God is identified with the spiritual sun, the sun's double that we see, and he has the power to take particular aspects.

Beings have a totally different concept of space and time and their joy, without being precise is frequently described as ineffable. Swedenborg let himself go, as all the clairvoyants, to an exaggeration of clairvoyance. He talked with angels, with demons and repeatedly, "the Lord appeared to him in an angelic form."

The clairvoyance's exaggeration is found among those who have claimed to enter the spiritual world. But we can perhaps discern the truth from the common and likely share that we find in these unverifiable explorations. Buddhists, and from them, the theosophists, speak about communities, meetings of beings, grouped together for love exchanges. Mr. Leadbeater along with many spiritualists, assign to these communities, human occupations to human. Mr. Caslant has summarized the descriptions of the spiritual world made by a large number of clairvoyants and his study is, of all, the most rigorous and most convincing. One is struck by the consistency of the accounts. These testimonies give the sensation of an environment of more intense vibrations, a disconcerting atmosphere for us and we often distinguish there, a painting that must be true. There are too many dazzling lights, sweet smells, harmonious sounds. As in all the images of the sky, we feel that if we entered into that sky, we would be seized by a divine disgust, but deep. The clairvoyants must all know the spiritualist religion and they add its rigorous moral to the tables they have glimpsed. One has the feeling that they could not resist adding price distribution wreaths and tawdry halos to the pious virgins and to soldiers who died for their country.

— "We are only, it is said in a communication, by a being who has reached the spiritual world, an ovoid light, more or less colored. I recognize the forms that I see around me, by their light, by their contour and by the memory mentioned by them."

Mr. Caslant say with reason: "Souls have no proper form. The entities take the following successive aspects as they attain regions increasingly high. Ghost or cloudy vapor, bright light or light head with a luminous trail of comet appearance, spearhead flame, radiant ovoid, gems, light dots*."

The one who, in virtue of a rare gift, has the possibility to penetrate the spiritual world, must first and foremost strip himself of any belief and of any preconceived idea. He enters in a world where thought is creative. If he searches there the confirmation of the catholic religion, as Swedenborg, he finds it there, without it being nothing convincing. He sees cities, houses, churches where monks sing, libraries where are sitting studious men, and he concludes of it that the spiritual world is an exact reproduction of the terrestrial world, in a subtler matter. He has seen in reality the imaginary creations of the deceased. It is the life of these dreams which allowed the spirits so many childish affirmations and also this pleasant painting of the afterlife where the one who dies sees himself surrounded by all his ancestors and deceased friends smiling and hands outstretched, in a similar landscape to the one he lived in, under a soft light of convention.

The spiritual world is a kind of opposite to the physical world. It is ruled by the same laws, but under their opposite aspect. When one has,

---

* Contemporary notebooks, *La vie après la mort*. Answers by Mr. E. CASLANT.

by his nature, the possibility to vibrate there in unison, one has lost all possibility to communicate with the physical world. The deceased who have reached this world, that is to say who were the most elevated among the living, cannot come back down, as so many people believe it, stricken in tables, incorporate in the physical form of seers.

The most disturbing law for us is the speed of the modification. The matter immobilizes. The condensation of the physical world only allows a slow modification. In the spiritual world, it is fast. But as this speed afflicts us on earth because it takes the shape of decrepitude, it is a cause of delight in the spiritual world. The delight comes from the development. The exchanges of thought and affection are made naturally with other beings by the game of the surrounding life, by the creation of these communities that have glimpsed all the scrutinizers of the life of the spirit.

These communities are in a perpetual activity. But this activity is different from ours, an ecstatic activity. It does not manifest by movements. It is similar to the activity of man on earth who feels a growth joy by reading a book. In these communities, those who loved each other on earth and who found each other, know by the intimate combination of their spiritual substance, a delight of which the old spasm of the body was only a miserable foretaste. They unite completely by the communion of their fluids, thus they had of it once the presentment, but their physical forms no longer constitute barriers between them. According to their development, according to their faculty of expansion, they join with creatures of their community who have the closest affinities with them. They see fall the separation caused by jealousy. Their enjoyment is all the greater as they merge with more numerous creatures. Their intelligence expands by the contribution of the experiences of others which become by this communion their own experience. And this expansion is constantly growing.

Inferior beings, limited by the shell of their selfishness, they barely transform by the passage of death. They come back towards earth, nearly similar to themselves. Those who know the delight of modification, receive in the spiritual life a speed acceleration they communicate to those they love and train, almost despite them, by the vertigo of their love.

All races end. All momentums die, in proportion to the power generated at the beginning. The one who has penetrated in the spiritual life with the immoderate love of himself, feels, at some point, the perception that he is going to lose himself in the collective unity of his phalanx. Then his strength of expansion stops. His selfishness gets back on top. He will no more be able to continue to love without ceasing to remain himself. Beside him, there will be more vigorous organisms which will not lose their own nature, by the continual game of effusion. The being is taken by the consciousness of his selfishness and with it reappears the desire of the matter which is its confirmation. In front of the danger of dispersal, he will aspire to incarnate.

And this is the great formidable or sublime turning.

The necessity to become God by metamorphosis

The Buddha admitted that there were six paths in which we were brought by birth and four ways by which accomplished this birth.

"The six paths are the conditions of Deva, Asura, man, Preta, animal and inhabitants of hells*. The four ways by which accomplishes the birth are: the humidity, an egg, a matrix, a metamorphosis†."

Thus a solemn minute will come when I shall be born. The door of birth is as inexorable as the door of death. But will I have the choice between the births? Among the conditions that the Buddha enumerates which one I will have the right and power to choose? I know that thanks to my lack of remorse I will not be an inhabitant of hells. I have no sufficient coarse desires to be attracted by an animal form. I developed enough my intelligence in order not to become this miserable ghost the Preta is.

Undoubtedly, all I gathered with pride of thoughts, of admirations, of hopes, to make of it a particular personality, will join bundle, animated by the taste of life. The light of my desire will make me know that I need a man's body to satisfy myself. I will not incarnate by the humidity as the worms, I will not incarnate by the egg as some animals, I will discover will ability the human matrix.

This female matrix is the common door of my species. But in what extent can I hope to find a better birth? Who knows if the determination with which I model my soul will not move me aside from the inner incarnation of the earth and will not allow me to transform by a metamorphosis?

For it is by the metamorphosis that the man becomes a Deva. These

---

* The Deva is a being higher than the man in the hierarchy of beings. The Asura is a being higher than the man but which uses his elevation to develop its selfishness. The Preta is a sort of vegetative ghost inferior to the animal. The state of Preta is attained by refusing to develop one's intelligence.

† BURNOUF, *Histoire du Bouddhisme indien.*

Devas are also called gods. They constitute the degree which, in the scale of beings, is immediately placed above the man. So restricted our perception is, we have the notion of a part of that scale. We see above ourselves the mineral, the vegetable, and the animal. We do not occupy the top of the scale. What encourages thoughtful little minds to believe it, is that the higher degrees are materially invisible and escape to our knowledge.

Despite the narrowness of the field experience, one can notice that the separation between reigns is grower as one arises. The stone and the vegetable are closely linked. The vegetable and the animal have intermediary species that participates to both reigns but they are more differentiated. From the animal to the man, the ring of the chain is looser. The separation is even greater from the man that the higher degree is invisible to him.

This is one of the mysteries of nature. It has multiplied the difficulties as we no more capacities to vanquish them. Gods are invisibles and yet we must believe in their existence. This faith is necessary to become one of them by the mysterious operation of the metamorphosis. The example of the caterpillar and the butterfly gives us a modest model of this change. Thus nature throws here and there, landmarks to make us understand its directions. It is our turn to discover the signs it has, by playing, left on the roads to guide us.

How this metamorphosis accomplishes in the immeasurable darkness of the afterlife? The insect is larva, then nymph and it is in the sleep that its embryonic cells liquefy and become a new, almost miraculous creation, a being dissimilar to the first, with wings to fly. The zoological science does not explain the intimate essence of transformation. The man is by the bye more complex than the insect. If the laws are the same from top to bottom of the scale, the metamorphosis must accomplish with great simplicity. The secret alchemy which is at its base is an alchemy of love. The transmutation must operate by virtue of the inner call.

The Hindus have thought that thousands of terrestrial incarnations, wonders of asceticism, superhuman power were necessary to attain the state of god. Many Greek philosophers have estimated that the practice of virtues, the daily wisdom conciliating with a moderate participation to the pleasures of life, were sufficient to allow man to attain the higher degree with a human state. Hindus or Greeks, which ones are right?

If it is the ascetic Buddhists, I will have to come back often on earth, stammer in childhoods, tolerate the human ugliness, mine and the one of others, assist to animal massacres, see triumph the ruthless mediocrity. With this idea, I am ceased by an immense discouragement.

But if it was the Greek sages who have attained the truth more closely, is it not an extraordinary audacity to rank among the best men, the elite of the wise and virtuous? Without any ostentatious exaggeration, I can say that I have not practiced the virtue, like these ancient philosophers, that I was selfish, I was eager for pleasures, all things which seem logically, to have brought me back on earth. I did with my desires a creation of which one will have to realize the effects.

A desire is killed by another one more powerful. We are in a prodigious ignorance of the quality of gods. The only certitude that we have about them is that the strength emitted to attain them draw us closer to them. The laws of nature are full of mystery. They make sometimes with no reason, extraordinary gifts. Regarding them, the modesty, the quality purely human, does not exist in any degree. A divine pretension is needed, aspired to the metamorphosis which will make us god. An exaggerated modesty could drove us back to being animal. Ask a lot so that a lot is given to us.

And the laws are blind which can be, if not defeated, at least cleverly diverted. We see streams overthrowing trees, rolling boulders with inexorable fury. The trickery of men, manifesting by patient works, manages to capture their strength. The laws do not choose between the merits. Like the streams, they rush into the place we have dug for them.

But an inner wisdom tells me that there cannot be a metamorphosis without the precipitation of a spiritual seed. I have to attain during my man's life to assimilate some bits of the nature of the gods. I have to steal them a thought, a though with its wings and its multicolored flame to shape it within me, make of it a double with wings and a multicolored flame.

And when this thought will be mine, assimilated to the substance of my soul, perhaps will I be taken, as Perseus on Bellerophon, as Sigurd on the swan, towards the worlds of divine thoughts.

But the task is not easy. One has to know the unknowable nature of gods. Where could I learn it? How could I cease a divine thought? Should one look at the stars or scrutinize the essence of the matter? Should one become a physicist, analyze the electrons with the most complicated devices or simply sit on a balcony, on a summer's night and consider the space with a quiet heart? How to discover the intimate essence of the gods to participate in their lives?

Devas, Angels and Demons

It is only since the advent of the new idol, science, that men have ceased to admit the existence of higher spiritual intelligence than human intelligence. Human pride in developing refused to conceive that the man was not at the top of the hierarchy of creatures in the universe. This error has become an absolute dogma, even for occultism and theosophy. Visible worlds are created, according to them, for the perfection of the man. The man has no other future than to become perfect under the name of adept. The aim is not to escape from humanity but to reach the illusory top.

Yet all ancient religions and all ancient sages had put man in his place. We knew that immediately existed above him a hierarchy and that the ideal was to reach it. It was the Devas among Hindus, the Feristahs among Zoroastrians, the Demons and Gods among Greeks, the Angels and Archangels among Jews, Christians and Muslims.

These nouns however do not designate the same beings, in an absolute way.

Devas, in a certain sense given to this word, are the souls of the elements. There is a Deva of fire, another of water, and so for each element. Deva also means the state in which one finds himself after passing the human state.

Christians think that all men who have made their salvation become angels after death. These angels take a man in their custody, follow all his actions and even his thoughts and protect him to the extent that the man let himself be protected. They are the guardian angels. I have often thought of the miserable state in which these superior creatures would be if such a thankless task entrusted to them. To witness the life of a man, his mediocre concerns and meanness and also only have such a low power of control! Hell as it is described would almost be preferable. But perhaps that the angelic state develops charity qualities that give patience and make accomplish in joy this melancholic surveillance. May the order of things, through immeasurable futures, never grant me the necessary charity to become a guardian angel!

Besides, if each man was followed and advised at all times by a special angel, he would eventually lose all freedom, the angel being infinitely superior to him and having in the long run to infuse him his will. A familiar communication would establish. The function of the angel being to help, he would like nothing better than to rush and advise when there would be a call. However, this communication occurs only in rare cases.

The Greeks have been the closest to the truth. They knew that men could achieve after death, by the perfection of their lives, to a higher state. They called them then, geniuses or glorified hero. The word demon had for them a broader sense. It designated in general, an invisible spirit, a power manifested only by thought, of human order or not.

The best known demon is the one of Socrates. He manifested himself to this wise as an inner voice or by visible signs for his eyes. Socrates has often talked about it to his disciples and he complied his actions to the demon's instructions. This demon was a special being who had his preferences and antipathies since he gave to Socrates advice for some of his friends and remained obstinately silent when it came to other friends he did not like. He sees a design to him of the human life and judged the policy despicable, at least for a philosopher, since he turned Socrates and directed him toward the study of wisdom.

Many philosophers who have studied this demon concluded that it was not an external being to Socrates. According to them, the voice where the signs would have been produced by the inner and omniscient thought of Socrates, what is now called the unconscious, this unconscious with which explains one explains everything, to avoid the trouble of finding and believing further. They were wrong. The evidence is in the very special way he gave his opinions. He never said to do one thing rather than another. He exhorted not to make an action he deemed bad. He conformed himself in this way to a universal law of intelligence that forces the intelligent to respect the freedom of others, not to enter the chain of causes and effects that are its own.

This demon had naturally only a limited power. On several occasions, he had given opinions that helped protect Socrates of life. It seems that he did not gave them, to protect him from the Athenian court which condemned him. Maybe he did not foresee what was going to happen. Men are always tempted to believe that a power coming from an invisible world is necessarily unlimited. It is not so. The more the beings are spiritually higher and the more it is difficult for them to get into the material domain to alter its facts. Human thoughts have become alien to them and represent for them a distasteful element they do not penetrate without oppression. To high men correspond high demons. The one of Socrates was to be one of those, and as such, he would neither have been able nor he would have known to influence the accuser Meletus. Such interventions must, moreover, be prodigiously exceptional. Then the death of Socrates perhaps constituted for the demon a way to find a friend in a form similar to his. Socrates thought himself that death was a happy event, a deliverance, when it came at the favorable and harmonious minute set by fate.

Plato, like his master Socrates, estimated that demons were aware geniuses, intermediaries between the man and the higher essences which thought animated the universe. Below the divine soul, were secondary deities, one embodied in the stars, others in cosmic forces, such as the elements.

The demons formed a hierarchy below these powers and the human souls occupied a lower degree. All these creatures were changing nature, tended toward the universal, or went down to the particular. The wisdom of antiquity and then Christianity, with its heavenly hosts and its overlays of seraphim have only complied with the belief of the divine Plato.

Many wise and many foolish have been visited by demons who have gave them advice, almost always in their interest and which sometimes were bad advice according to the human reason. The best known geniuses were those of Paracelsus, and of the physician and astrologer Cardano. Many Catholic saints have been visited by superior beings they called angels. It is not surprising that mostly men leading an ascetic life have been visited by these genies. Such a presence comes usually from a relationship in a previous life with a being that has surpassed the human stage. It is the sign of mutual aid of a former companion who, in the limited extent it when it is possible to him, provides guidance to the one who remained in the terrestrial shadows. One can never expect from him an advice on material benefit. Because the material benefit is a link between you and life and is not an advantage for the one who has the spiritual sight.

But there will never be communication without trust. Trust is a force. It fosters the illusion, but it also produces a living reality. An absolute trust in the existence of gods is necessary to communicate with them. In terms of gods, trust is a material element, visible with its own color and resonance, it is through the channel of that element that a report can be established. Trust is furthermore not insufficient. Many fools who have trusted always had on their heads empty and silent heavens. But just as it takes water to navigate, fire to heat food, it is necessary to be certain that gods exist to acquire that proof, by brief reports.

The one who does not believe, will only meet men during his lifetime. He will also meet only men when he will pass the threshold of death, whether he is plunged in the darkness or the awakening of his consciousness gives him the benefit of any light. The world of the afterlife is still a human world, its confers no special knowledge, no vision of the past or the future. The mediocre man stays mediocre there. The intelligent only has there the intelligence he has amassed. The supraterrestrial beings evolve in other spheres. In order that the man comes to contact with them, either during the life or after death, the salutation that allows to contact them must contain its syllables the certainty that they exist and the faith that one can reach them.

Method to communicate with the Gods

It is possible to talk with gods or rather to receive of it inspirations after having called them. Gods do not possess a body similar to ours and this is why the communication between them and us is so difficult. They express themselves by materializing a voice, what must be a difficult task since there is no example of long speeches pronounced by them. They try to make understand their thoughts either by some monosyllables or by a geometric sign, either rather by an image. The vague portrait of someone having existed must be the most convenient way to express oneself because it is the one that they use most of the time.

The invisible world is around us, beating of a prodigious life, though different from ours and if we perceive nothing of it, it means that we do not listen, we do not look carefully enough with our inner senses. If we were more prepared to hear and see, perhaps would we have the revelation of a crowd of hidden things, infinitely passionate. We would be disappointed regarding the future. Because as powerful as Devas and demons are, they can only know with certainty the part of the future of which the causes are generated and that no human liberty will come to hinder. And if their prevision is the announcement of a danger, this prevision will only realize if ones does not trust them, because if one trusts, one will do what is needed to avoid the danger and then the prevision will be false.

We can only communicate with gods by elevating towards them and where more or less temporary when we reach them. The possibility to reach them has sometimes the duration of a lightning. The artistic emotions, when they do not loose themselves in the sensuality make us glimpse brief lights of divine order. How to analyze this world where everything is order and beauty and where the highest human qualities are not represented by facial expressions or body lines? What do we glimpse in these brief passages where we have been thrown by the burst of a harmony, the rapid rocket of a thought? Are we in the presence of radiant landscapes, architectures of temples more perfect than have created the geometries of men? Is the ideal satisfaction that one feels coming from a vaster power of creation, from the projection of oneself, or from the endured flow of a subtler universe of which the beauty is subject to more complex laws and which discovery throws you in the rapture? This is the world of the gods. Those who live there of a constant have to suffer to get out, even for a brief time and endure the pain of a form integration, so fleeting it may be.

To communicate with the gods, one must first put himself in harmony with their thoughts. Yet, the currents of their thoughts are almost always backwards to ours. Our bodies which are so precious to us and to which ugliness we are used to, seem to them caricatural and of an odious weight. They consider as property the destruction of these forms in which souls are captive and they wish for those they love, a rapid and liberating death. Our prayers for the extension of our life are heard as manifestations of our stupidity. They have of the rest no more power to make us live than to make us die but their love makes them wish our death.

Gods hardly perceive the actions and they only grant them importance insofar as they are the symbol of thoughts. All the movements of the matter are confused to them, whereas the smallest thoughts are luminous. Crimes only exist in the intention, since the result is almost always favorable, especially if the crime is exerted against someone very developed who is not expected to be reincarnated. In this case, they perceive a bad intention which has a happy result.

They also conceive differently what we call good works. Good works, accomplished with a sincere love for life links the man who makes them to the one who receives them and increases the love for life of both of them. They both enchain themselves hereby to the terrestrial life. In this way the good works have a bad result. They feel its pure intention, but they are distressed by the delay they cause. Everything is relative, naturally, to each individual and to his development. But while in men, even for the most intelligent, we judge according to the differences of fortune, the acquired titles, the education, the way to eat and dress, among gods these differences are no more noticeable and men are known as lights more or less bright, according to the differences of intelligence or capacity for love.

It is because of such large differences in the comprehension of the world and that of souls, that it is difficult for us to communicate with the gods. We are not in tune with their thoughts. They experience, to get through to us, the same difficulty that we could have if we wanted to talk to a fish. Our inability to create a thought in the subjective world makes us consider by them, as silent and limited as the aquatic being with his silence and his dead eyes. But as we come to some conversations with the higher animals like the dog, likewise the gods come to communicate partially with the highest men.

The one wants to win the favor of their friendship must call them. The call expressed at random is not heard. One must know whom he is calling. Account must be taken that the gods do not stroll solitary in their relative space. They form groups. The more they are advanced in perfection the more they are numerous in their groups. We do not realize on the land similar groups of more than two. I speak about groups where one is intimately united. A link of physical pleasure, recent or old, is necessary to cement these tiny groups and they often break when physical pleasure ceases. We even find it difficult to conceive a profound union with many individuals. Among beings who have exceeded the human condition and are moving towards unity, the union is the law and they take wonderful delight of their mutual love.

Yet, by our physical constitution and especially our moral abilities we have affinities with certain groups. It is of one of them that we could receive relief. But how to know and to call them? Mrs. Annie Besant in an interesting study of the Devas said: "Every man is correlated with a specific manifestation of God. It is difficult for a man to discern to what god he is linked to." And at the moment when the reader thinks that a way is going to be revealed for this so important discernment, she adds: "I have no time to dwell on that point*." I do not know if,

* Annie Besant, *Evolution of Life and Form.*

at other times, she found the time, but I have not found in her works the valuable method allowing the man to discern the God of its own. It should be noted with melancholy that the greatest minds slip away when their speech will be revealing, either because they have indeed more pressing concerns, or because the secrets they will tell cannot be revealed to the miserable crowd of readers, or rather because they are unaware of the solution.

It is useless to seek the name of gods to invoke them. The gods have no name. The name disappears with the form at the time of death. It is significant that the names are always forgotten in spirit communications. This oversight may even be a feature of the truth of these communications. The name is the symbol of the personality of what separated it has. The more the mind rises, the more the separation is abolished and the name loses its meaning. A God who would have a name would not be a true God and wanting to give him a name that would be his own would be a sign of incomprehension.

The divine groupings must be formed by the attraction of a similar quality. There must be groups that have the purpose of music, or rather the power to improve themselves through music. Other groups are formed by the common intoxication of philosophy or that of mathematics. In the last case, for example, the best mode of the call is to fix his thought on the highest geometric form that we know and on the need to draw it. The union of beings is the general principle, but as it is common to all, a call made to the quality of love will spread and will not be effective.

The voice has a power of resonance which, when accompanied by the thought communicates to the plane of the mind. The one wants to communicate with the superior intelligences must orally formulate brief call of words, he will compose himself and where will be named the essential quality of the group to which it is addressed.

The words in order to jump materially need the ambient silence and deserve to be pronounced when the sun sets, in harmony with the breath of the earth, or at sunrise when the atmosphere has its maximum purity. Loneliness, lack of noise, and the air quality of the mountains are favorable to their flight. But the one who has the opportunity to set his thought strongly on a high ideal, can pronounce them without getting one's lips wet, in any place, even in the middle of a crowd, for words are only an accessory to help and only matters the thought.

The one whose mind is powerful and directs it to a high virtue which he has in him a reflection, receives the help he asks for from the fraternal hierarchy to which he addresses himself. But he must have the similar reflection, the piece of light so small it is, whose attraction allows the influx of the greater light. So he sets in motion a law similar to that of communicating vases. The prayers of ignorant believers who invoke deities, are only clumsy attempts for the implementation of this law. Believers have the marvelous element of trust, but they delay the help that would bring them in some instances, superior intelligences, by making a coarse physical representation of these intelligences with statues or images and by showing an abject humility.

The humility that manifests in the different forms of devotion, is the negation of what is asked. The pious lowering the religions acquire, that worship that is custom in India to provide to gurus and masters, the intellectual servitude in which these masters holds you, are the strongest barriers that separates men from gods. Besides, I have trouble believing that the real masters ask their disciples the pious fervor spoken of, and their infertile servility.

Gods are more perfect brothers. They can only speak to men if the fraternal relationship has been established, in virtue of an equality on one point. How would they need the same marks of respect as the rich men or men socially important? The genuflections, the dust kissing, the prostrations in front of statues, are confessions of ignorance and spiritual ugliness. The one who calls under that form, affirms in the same time that he will not be heard, that he does not deserve an answer.

The one who does not deserve one must not ask for it. Besides, he does not receive one. There is no link with the Gods only to receive what one already has a parcel of. Gods do not grant happiness as we conceive it. They do not have that happiness. They cannot even brush its elements. The most humanly commendable wishes, such as the one of a mother praying for the health of her child, of a soldier whishing the victory of his country, are not heard by them. What they can grant us is of another order, but it is the essential richness. The man who manages to make contact with the group where dominates the virtue he has cultivated, will receive this virtue in unexpected proportions. A foreign virtue is not brought to him by an unjust gift, if he has not cultivated within him its seed. The one of whom it is said that he is loved by gods is the one who has loved himself enough for having developed some divine in him. The musician will usefully call invisible musicians whose orchestras have ten thousand instruments and which will reveal incomparable sounds. The architect besotted by edifices will find lost laws of construction whose input will perhaps come from builders of Nineveh and of Babylon or more ancient cities erected on lost planets. The more the quality will be of a higher order the more it will be given with abundance. The one who will ask to love all beings will receive a torrent of love of which the flood will increase. And this gift is not made with a generosity of human order, but by an obligation of fraternity.

Prayers to the Gods

Oh nameless God, faceless God, you who see the earth as a pile of purple ashes and who perceive in the space unknown planets to men!

I address you standing, not out of pride, but because the drop of truth with which I got drunk myself taught me that the marks of respect were in your eyes only human faces and that the first condition to ask the intelligence is to judge oneself worthy of it.

I do not climb a high mountain to speak to you. I would then speak to you rarely. I address you in hotel rooms, on roads, in gardens, everywhere where I can press on my chest a fragment of beautiful silence. I am trying to project my thought towards you, as a fragile light, but that the power of hope prevents from trembling.

I cannot help but to look at the stars when I speak to you and I even think confusedly that you cannot hear me if I cannot see them. I know that you are not above than you are lower, but it is an illusion to which I am attached to think that the blue of the sky is the color of the pure spirit and that to the geometry of the stars corresponds the laws of the world.

I have sometimes the weakness to desire you being more human. I would not hate then to see you in a form similar to mine though slightly taller by the height, wearing Hindu dresses and those large fur hats worn in Tibet and which give such majesty.

I envy then those who obey rites. I would like to sing hymns, breathe the incense, pray Krishna or this virgin we see in all religions and that, if it was necessary, I would call Mary. Although I do not like much young children, I would be tempted to kneel before the one who is represented in a manger, the one who was recognized by the donkey and the bullock, especially because he was recognized by the donkey and the bullock.

But I realize that by kneeling, the heart is closer to the earth and that it is necessary to crawl as the snake to worship with perfection. Oh shapeless God, oh faceless God, keep the attributes of the invisible so that my soul goes up to you!

Oh God you who are all intelligence, give me the daily intelligence. Free me from the superstition which creates fear and from the instinctive courage which blindly fills. Give me the comprehension, the one of the fury of men, that of the resignation of animals, that of all the living souls.

Oh God you who are all measure, give me the knowledge of good and evil, of the power that spiritualizes and the strength which material-izes. Show me by a traced sign on a wall or in the clouds which side and the real good. Because daily events are filled with traps and it is often difficult to recognize those who leads to the spirit and those who keep away from it.

Oh God you who are all love, make me love creatures despite their ugliness, despite their foolishness. I know that beauty makes cry, but one should not have confidence in the gentleness of these tears. I know that the good and pure ones have often a nose too long and a ridiculous stomach. Free me from the disgust caused by the meanness and prevent me from running away when I see the smile of envy.

Oh God you who are all wisdom, will you have enough power to act on my inferior nature? Under the seven ostentatious sails of the quali-ties, I parry myself; there is a hard bark of stone and in it is found a cell of selfishness, more solid than the diamond. In this cell is hidden, in the form of a spark, a prodigious love of the terrestrial life that no wisdom can extinguish.

Oh shapeless God, oh faceless God, free me from the temptation of having a form, from the temptation of having a face. I wonder some-times if my desire to reach you is as sincere as I think. Aren't there two sincerities, that of its ideal and of oneself?

Oh God you who do not reign on earth and who cannot sit anyone down at your right, grant me some light, when the darkness of death will come. Help me keep my luminous consciousness as an eternal lamp. Free me from the weight so that I be light, from the desire so that I be pure, from the separation so that enjoy the presences. Teach me the secret of the metamorphosis so that I become similar to you.

Of the artificial creation of a Goddess

This happened at a time when I was recovering from a serious illness. Perhaps did death come near me without my knowledge. I did not notice it. It is possible that it was discreet. This is one of the qualities of death to go invisible when it approaches. Some people around me had sensed its presence and by poorly disguised anxiety, exaggerated solicitude had let me understand this feeling. I smiled, attributing to their pessimism, the fear of a coming which I thought secretly unlikely. Because a certain number of fools, I was part of during these few days, thought that they were, in the depths of themselves, physically immortal.

Because of the weakness of my body, my mind no longer enjoyed the same weighting qualities. My ideas succeeded each other with great rapidity and I was, on a continual way, in a light and fairly sweet intoxication. None of those severities which I have heard of mingled with it, which force to make wills or pronounce moving and solemn words. Life seemed coated me in a pleasant but unimportant beauty. Poems forgotten for years came back to my mind with strange book projects unfolding before me to be soon forgotten.

Yet suddenly I remembered a book that I read recently and which passage had pretty much impressed me. It was the book where Mrs. David Neel recounts her journey to Tibet. During this famous journey, she stopped on a mountain, in a hermit's hut; to practice meditation there according to the ancient methods of Tibetans lamas. Mrs. David Neel who received the gift of patience and rarest gift to fix her thought, obtained an extraordinary result.

After months of constant thought, she came to create a being of which she had represented the image to herself. She created the appearance and the contour of someone who became her companion in her solitude and who, when she stopped thinking about him, persisted in the existence to the point of becoming an obsession, she could not get rid of.

Mrs. David Neel, being prey to the wind and the snow of the Himalayas, could have created, which would have been as easy to her, an entertaining character who would have charmed her hours, some delicious dancer, a guitar player. She preferred to give birth to a dark hermit, severe lama in meditation. To an ideal austerity suits an austere achievement.

— Why, I told myself, wouldn't I try to imitate Mrs. David Neel? No doubt the disease brings a decline of principle because my friends come to me rarely and, if they come, it is always a little ahead of urgent appointments that make them leave me quickly. Reading makes me tired and I have long unoccupied hours. It would be an inestimable advantage to create a companion, visible to me alone, devoid of matter and which could be rich in beauty.

I immediately decided that the character of whom I was going to attempt the creation, would be of female sex. I considered that the grace of the face and body perfection were much better for the long interviews to the severity of an old lama. I instantly began to work with great enthusiasm and a half patience. It is is the sharpness of the image that we form to ourselves that contributes to the achievement. I stared forcefully before my eyes an ideal image of woman as beautiful as I could conceive her and like materials, I brought one by one my thoughts to bring her into existence out of the shadows of nothingness.

I was surprised by the relative speed with which I obtained a partial result. Certainly I was not claiming a desire to meditation such as that of Mrs. David Neel. But after a few days, when I called the image of this kind of goddess I had kneaded and painted according to my soul, I obtained a vision much more accurate than that provided by the effort of the ordinary imagination. I do not mean that the vision was an objective reality, far from it, but it encouraged me to devote more time to the work of creation, and I did it every night, by the light of a lamp which threw little light. I noticed that the creation was realized even better if the light was smaller and the room quieter.

Then something curious happened what threw me into astonishment.

The first draft of the goddess imagined in my mind had a very white skin, the size quite large and the features of a beauty akin to the Greek type. I had even looked at reproductions of statues, to comply the details of the hairstyle to the entire form. But the goddess appeared to me in a manner of speaking in spite of me, with a skin slightly tanned, of small size, a loose hair, gushing like thick sheaves and charged with bluish reflections to which I had not thought of. I tried, of course, to bring her back to my personal design. I especially tried to remove this hair which phosphorescent quality I did not like and which was too important to me by its excessive thriving. But the image decreased significantly of accuracy. She made rather good progress of reality as soon as I represented her to myself with unexpected attributes. Her features became clearer even more rapidly as my conscious will ceased to shape them. I soon saw a beautiful face, mobile, who easily passed from sadness to delight and did not resemble to any known face in my life.

From the beginning I had thought of giving her a name, a Greek name of course. It was in appearance very easy. I wanted the name to express a connection with the physical of the one that would carry it. I was obliged to reject all the names that stood in my mind and it clearly appeared to me that it was not a Greek name that I had to give her. The goddess who came out of the depths of my soul truly belonged to a particular race, an Eastern race that I could not define precisely, but that had nothing to do with the Greek race.

Something even more singular has happened again. The creature with bluish hair showed, if not thoughts, at least instincts that I had not allowed her to demonstrate. She showed herself to some extent autonomous. Instead of waiting to be called, she happened to appear at times chosen by her and not by me, and even with some malignancy she came at the least appropriate times to her coming.

One of my friends, a particularly serious and wise man, came sometimes at five o'clock to talk to me of the highest problems concerning death and human destiny. Hardly the conversation was engaged as the goddess started to wander around the room, she smiled at me over his head, made flourish the circle of her hair or casually stretched herself on the bed. I sincerely whished then her disappearance but my will was powerless to dispel her.

Our relation was strictly chaste, but I understood that it could be different and it only depended on me. I had created the goddess to have before the eyes a vision of human beauty destined to develop in me a state of spiritual love and high thoughts. I perceived that there was in the body movements of the goddess, in the expression of his face, a voluptuous contribution in which I had nothing to do with, that was absolutely exterior. I had, after some time, a companion whose reality was growing, in which I sensed a charming soul but subject to human passions and whose essence, coming originally from me, became more and more foreign to me.

Mrs. David Neel, said in her book, obsessed by the dark silhouette of her lama, she could not get rid of him abruptly. She was forced in order to remove him; to use the same methods she had used to create him. But I could not bring myself to remove a creature so gently alive, so gently fugitive, who had a so particular personality and whose smile even expressed, sometimes, to me, an irony without malice. I wonder, however, if I could have done that.

It happened that I overcame my illness. I began to go out again and there was a form of concentration which was abolished for me. No doubt, on entering the room where the goddess had become accustomed to live, I brought back foreign spiritual elements which were contrary to her. She became vaguer, her presence was inconclusive. I cannot say that she was sad to disappear, although I seemed to discern in her a certain melancholy. But who knows if that melancholy was not the reflection of the one I felt by losing her?

Of what substance was made this being without a matter? I am forced to think, despite the improbability that this represent, that she wasn't only created by me. Perhaps have I only created the spiritual mold where an instinctive being and owner of an infinitesimal particle of consciousness came to live by friendship or by simple taste for life?

Even if her obedience wasn't always absolute, I have to give evidence of her qualities of docility, of charm and affection. I was especially sensitive to a way of joyful and poetic fantasy that manifested by attitudes and smiles. But from where did this amazing hair with blue phosphorescence as it was never given to me to see on a human head come from?

I have never been able to give a name to the silent friend of my nights of convalescence. All those who have presented themselves to my mind have been immediately rejected as false names. I sometimes regret it because there is a power in the name and I imagine that through the magic of syllables, I could make suddenly come back the missing goddess.

I desire it sometimes, especially when comes the dusk, when I am alone and that the lamp only throws a low light. I have called her sometimes but it was always in vain. Yet, I know that she is not dead, that she exists somewhere and that an invisible link bounds her to me. Perhaps is she resting in the stay of power beauties and archetypes of what yet does not exist? Perhaps is she in the need for her half existence of the atmosphere of sickness and has she only her fullness of life with her creator's death? Perhaps will she only appear to me at the minute of my death? Perhaps have I long days to spend in her company? I turn around sometimes with the feeling that she is behind me. I would not be surprised to see her, one day, sit peacefully next to me in a familiar posture.

I have only reported the coming and disappearing of this goddess as an example showing that there is a great variety of different gods who live in our atmosphere. Some are higher than us and others are inferior to us. We can give the life to ones by the use of our forces that we ignore. There are others who could be useful to us in many ways if we knew how to call them and share our wish with them.

Thus would we be driving ourselves regarding beings less developed. We hardly take care of ants or turtles,—I am quoting species randomly—and of their spiritual growth. But if an ant or a turtle would come to us begging and would manage to make us understand that it is waiting for a moral help from us, most of the average men would do as much as impossible to help it. It is from the hierarchy immediately placed above the man that we can hope for a decisive help. It is by passing through the door of death that we have the opportunity to make a big step forward. We also have the risk to step backwards. We must prepare ourselves during our lifetime for this passage, which can be joyful but also sad, to become profitable and so that we no longer have to cross again this door that rotates so unexpectedly and of which the hinges by turning, make a mysterious noise.

The energy of perfection
and the message of the Nightingale

As a young girl dressed in white who enters a banquet hall where are sitting coarse men, thus the spirit enters one day in the middle of the desires of the soul. Rude men laugh with concupiscence; some invite the girl to sit on their knees; others make the gesture of grasping her slender waist. The most perverse secretly meditate. They think it would not be enough to spill the contents of their glass in her throat and spread her hair on the table. They would want to make her participate in their downfall. Because it is a pain for rude men to feel that there is an ideal beauty of which they will never brush the immaculate dress.

The desires of the soul are the same and act regarding the white young girl as if they had an autonomous will. They are trying to pervert the mind. But once it entered the banquet room, the bottles fall of it selves and the laughter of the drinkers turns into stuttering. Some are paralyzed. Others fell to their knees and seek in their memory prayer phrases. And there comes a time when one of them grabs a torch and lit the room's paneling. So the beard and the cloths of coarse men ignite, they transfigure themselves in the fire and they become like splendid Buddhas.

The transformation by the spirit must take place before the death.

— Every man must begin by making himself attractive and divine to get the view of the beautiful and of the divinity, said Plotinus.

The one wants to live with the gods after death must at least have glimpsed them during his terrestrial life. The one who does not believe will not see them, but he will have the possibility to conform himself to the divine and develop, even though more slowly than the one who believes, the elements by which he will be able to enter the higher worlds.

In the air we breathe there is a kind of invisible energy that we can call the energy of perfection. This energy, infinitely subtle, can be received by any man. But some have more facilities than others because they are better conditioned to receive this energy. They are modeled to be better receiving devices.

This energy has no physical manifestation. Its vibration mode must be the one of the spiritual world. It is in virtue of the possession of a fragment of this energy that artists create a certain quality of art works of, works that tend to perfect the soul. A very large number of artistic works, among the most admired, are not aroused by the energy of perfection, including those which develop sensuality and love of pleasure. Leonardo da Vinci, Michelangelo, Wagner, the poet Andersen, had been able to develop in them, consciously or unconsciously, the energy of perfection.

Nature that likes to throw in different realms, as an exception, the harbingers of subsequent reigns, has sown in plants and animals, a premature ability to receive and develop the energy of perfection. There is a particle in the sapphire and amethyst. This is why we attribute to the possession of these stones if they are perfect, some power to develop spirituality among the one who carries them. We can see that most sapphire or amethyst carriers do not have in them the slightest element of spirituality. It is that the force is incommunicable to the one who does not want to, nor who does not know how to receive it. It is not enough for the force to be projected; there must be a door through which it can pass. Moreover, the way of cutting the stones may reduce or even remove the expanding power of virtue they contain. It is in the raw state they have their greatest quality gift and the work we do to them, while promoting the brilliance, only weakens the power of expansion. It is for this reason that in China, many gems are preserved in the raw state.

There are plants to which was vested the power to store energy of perfection. Flowers, especially roses are sometimes the expression of that energy. What we call, in our ignorance, a tendency to good or a tendency to evil, already differentiates the plants. The unique spirit of each species transforms and flourishes in a direction clearly determined. There is a vegetable aristocracy of which we can measure the degrees by distinguishing among species the higher element they contain. The coffee plant and poppies have an intimate relationship with the intelligence and the imagination and men who engage with a wise measure to coffee or opium, can benefit from the power of perfection, transformed by the plant alchemy. These two plants represent the top attained through the effort of species of their reign. Some reasonable drunkenness of coffee or opium may involve the one who knew how to direct his drunkenness to the life in the higher worlds. If the absorption of coffee or opium does not always favor the use of thought to the earthly point of view, if their contribution is not what is known as practice, they give a fore-taste of trade of the man with the gods. Of them can be expected an expansion of the capacity to love and above all that rare, this invaluable momentum that invites us to exceed ourselves.

Other plants have these qualities in a lower degree, or have developed other spiritual qualities. The rosemary was able to capture some of the energy of perfection and it manifests it in the fragrance that it spreads when one crumples leaves in his hand. Then one feels by breathing it that there is a communication of the plant with the afterlife and that this communication is constant. It can be in some cases for the man, a path towards the spiritual life. Similarly the box tree, when its foliage is wet from the rain gives the intuition, if not the knowledge of death. Besides one should simply consider it to understand by its appearance that it is towards this order of wisdom that his soul is oriented.

Those who want to know the future should make experiments with the bay. The core of the bay produces an effort to conquer the qualities of divination. These qualities were known to the Greeks. The Pythia who prophesied in the temples were holding a bay branch in the hand and chewed of it a leaf by speaking.

But we do not know how to use the hidden divine properties in the lower realms. We have not tried to pierce the mystery plant. We only tried to extract from the plants only remedies for bodies. We did not ask them anything for the elevation of the soul. We never put them in contact with our intuition. There are probably many plants that pos-sess treasures of spirituality. But we do not know them. They should be discovered and their millennial effort enjoyed. As among men, the more modest must be the wisest. Similarly as there was not the slightest breath of power of perfection in Napoleon, he was fully human, and likewise there is little to expect, in this order of ideas, as the proud trees like the sycamore or the oak tree. They are fully plants. One must be content with their shade. But if we were able to love plants as they apply for it with the embrace of their branches and the curve of their leaves, we would discover those which are at the top of their hierarchies and whose soul has been able to achieve, by a secret way, the spiritual life.

It is the same for animals. There are some, such as bees, ants, beavers, who went much further than we in the development of certain qualities. It is only today that Mr. Maurice Maeterlinck began to draw deep conclusions from the study of their habits. The history of animals, if we could write it, would be the story of a long and systematic killing and the research to penetrate their minds would only have a small part of it.

The energy of perfection manifests itself with an extraordinary power in the personality of the nightingale. Such as sapphire by the light, the poppy by the juice, the rosemary by the smell, the nightingale manifests by the singing, the divine energy by which he is possessed. This energy is never silent. It has a need for expression.

This need is at its maximum level in the nightingale. The nightingale represents the highest point reached by the animal souls, in their effort toward the divine.

It seems that there are no bird concerns in the song of the nightingale. This song is not about broods, owl's beak fears, or delight in the warmth of a nest. There is no plumage shivers in it.

It is organized with more science than the anthem of a poet. It is more concise and ordered than a human music. It contains the last word of the genie which is the knowledge of correspondences of nature and of the soul. Not only of the soul of the nightingale and the human soul, but of all souls of the earth. It is a song that flies beyond the known limits where creatures can fly. And with it flies away we do not know where, the landscape where resounded the singing and the heavens which cover it. And the one who hears it, with the suitable reverence, during a calm spring night, is himself transported in a kind of spiritual fever, where the senses have nothing to do with it, towards another more beautiful world than the one we know.

The song does not give the vision of the other world. It indicates the way that leads to it. It says that it exists and it proves it by the mere fact that such a high and consoling thought is expressed by the voice of a bird.

And if we consider the enormous and unusual dimension of the voice in such a small being, if we think of the courage it takes to sing this tune by a spring night when the raptors birds, bearers of iron beaks and music carefree, prowl by trees, we will agree that there is a mystery in the nightingale and that only, a euphoria which is above all creation, the proclamation of a sublime message can motivate this exaltation of divine order.

It is possible that this is exclusively for the man that the message is sung to. The nightingale has an extreme ease to communicate with the man and answering his thoughts. In a country where there are many of these mysterious birds, I was able to establish relationships with them that only our mutual shyness has prevented him from being closer.

Many men were able to concentrate in themselves the energy of perfection. But they have turned it towards the inside of their souls to a quiet possession. No one has ever managed the perfect disinterestedness of the song proclaimed in the night, by the magnificent audacity of the nightingale. The animal kingdom has expressed religious and artistic impetus where have mingled the self-sacrifice and the great fervor, that has never been surpassed by men. There is here something disturbing and enigmatic.

But what arouses most astonishment is that the message seems to have been understood by no one. Birds are not influenced by the divine voice that fills the night. We do not see them making any tribute to the nightingale. The blackbird, warbler and other birds are not silent when he sings and even struggle to drown his voice by their mediocre songs. The owl enjoys the singer as well as the silent bird. Men listen to him only with a distracted ear. We do not see them gather piously under the tree where the message is proclaimed. Some are bothered because their sleep is disturbed by that too beautiful and too heartbreaking voice. I remember of a venerable and good character, but hunter, who said he had more pleasure out of eating the singing birds, even meager, than birds which did not sing.

A light has be lit in nature, which burns of an incomparable flame and that nobody sees, because the eyes are looking down, instead of looking up. A sound of divine essence resounds through the shadows of the earth and ears remain closed because each has plugged them with the lead of their disbelief. And those who believe are not more willing to listen. They sometimes given themselves some trouble to attain an illusory perfection. There are some who are in search of masters whose word will enlighten them. There are even some going in India and Tibet with the hope of finding those teachers.

And yet they only have to sit in the corner of a road, near a garden or along a wood, to hear, clear, understandable and in the form of the deepest expression, the message that teaches, in the darkness of night, the direction to be taken by the soul toward the light.

***

The Hindu yoga, the science of the breath, the meditation processes tend to the direct acquisition of perfection. But all these methods are unsuccessful, difficult and give little results because the one who employs them has not learned to conquer formerly, the energy of perfection.

All prescribed methods require as a first condition to make the silence of the mind, that is to say the interruption of all thoughts to reveal the flower of deep wisdom. Yet, this silence of the mind is very difficult to obtain. Memories rush en masse at the minute when one wants to get rid of them and if we reach a beginning of silence, there are often the apparitions of bizarre or grotesque images which have no relation with the deep wisdom. Breathing exercises that some can manage to do are annoying for others. They release unknown forces, they sometimes cause physical disorders and more often mental disorders. They put in a nervous state of agitation and repel those who volunteer.

There are for ordinary men — and it is always wise to place oneself in this broad category — more simple methods to acquire the energy of perfection. But their extreme simplicity will reject them, wrongly, by the proud ones. Yet these are the ones that will best allow to obtain an adequate knowledge of the higher worlds.

The first method is hearing noises coming out of a garden or a forest. One must choose, whenever possible, a place that is not disturbed by car or railway cries. These discordant cries are the expression of the retrograde force of the world, the one that goes towards the material enjoyment, instead of rising towards the spiritual order. They are at the opposite pole of the natural harmony and they paralyze it, such as the introduction of a large fair case in the performance of a symphony. One must also choose a garden where are gathered trees of different species, because the more species are numerous the more there are various vegetable souls which express themselves.

The wind, by passing through the leaves, tend to solve in harmonies plants meditations. Plants souls are less aware than ours, but they are less depressed that human souls in the materialization by the complication of organs and the appetite of the selfish separation. They undergo the law of descent, but they are closer to the spiritual life to the case. Their voice do not proclaim the immediate return to the mind, but the conformation to the laws of the world. For the vegetable soul has developed in the direction of wisdom. One must try to understand its voice, to abandon oneself to the plant currents that make run up through the space a hymn of wisdom.

There comes a time when one has the feeling of mingling with these currents and being carried away by them. This never happens immediately and the quality of trees has great importance. There are some who are proud and underdeveloped. Others that are closed to what is human and to which meditation it is impossible to participate. Some men have affinities with some trees rather than with others. I am inclined to believe that the love we have for a region comes mostly from the affinity we have with its vegetation. Pines, cypresses, eucalyptuses are great trees of great spirituality and those whose voice is most profitable.

But we must as far as possible choose a place with trees where no river passes. First, because the sound of the water — the one of a river or that of the sea — brings the soul to earth. Then, because the proximity of water causes the proximity of an entire animal people, toads, frogs, birds. All these creatures are making love calls, hunger cries, cries of fear. Those voices that are considered complementary to the voice of nature, take away by their material character any sublime expression to hymns of trees.

But no matter how pure the singing rising from various plant species is, to discover its meaning, differentiate it from other voices of nature, such as the rough voice of the sea, one must have a special soul and the quality of the song is relative to the quality of the one who is listening it.

Another method is the careful contemplation of the night sky, when the stars are clearly visible. No one, or almost no one, looks at the sky. Yet one remembers of its view, a useful lesson at the effort of the perfection, a force of heart that secretly infiltrates, without the rational thought having anything to do with it. One must look at the sky when there are no clouds and no moon. The light of the moon draws back to terrestrial dreams, images relating to the generation, to the pleasures of the senses. The perfection of energy comes from the color of the immensity of the figures traced by the stars and of their geometrical disorder.

It is vain for the one who wants to raise his soul by heaven, to calculate distances, to speculate the relativity of space or other problems of such order. The examination of these problems is fruitful in itself, but it is of another order. It leads to a valuable expansion of intelligence. It is not used to acquire the energy of perfection. This energy penetrates the being in other ways. The contemplation of the sky and of its stars leads to a kind of semi-trance during which the soul is receptive and absorbs the energy of perfection.

And when one receives it, as for all really precious wealth, one does not know that he receives it.

Forecast of death

A certain number of men are informed of their impending death. It is a precious favor. Knowing in advance the date of their end, they can accomplish a few key actions, gather around them some useful thoughts. Thus they are guaranteed a lot of anguish in the afterlife. They do not have the risk of a sudden awakening with remorse for not having done one of these expensive projects that one always puts in the last hour. Blessed are those who are informed of their impending death.

In order to have the prediction of one's death, one must have an enlightened soul through meditation or be linked to a group. When one has meditated for a long time, one has gained some clairvoyance on all of its destiny and can be provided by its internal knowledge the moment of the passage from one world to the other. But if for various reasons the soul remains devoid of clairvoyance, it happens that the beings of the group to which one is linked, compensate for the missing clairvoyance. The forecast then occurs not by an intimate intuition, but by an exterior sign.

This sign is usually the hearing of a music of transcendental order heard by the one whose death is near. Many examples of it were recorded in books written about that subject. Latu, disciple of Ramakrishna, was warned of his own death by the sound of a flute. Music has often then a call character. Many families have traditionally an announcement of the death of each of their members by the hearing of a funeral march and this funeral march has been heard by people who did not belong to the family. The sign is sometimes, instead of music, the appearance of a form, which is usually that of a relative or friend.

There must be many cases where the forecast, when it comes from beings of the afterlife, cannot be made, whatever the good will of these beings. Their knowledge of causes and effects is hardly less limited than ours, and the more they belong to a higher hierarchy, the more things of the earth are obscure for them. Physical disintegration is exercised in the molecules of the body long before the moment of death. This disintegration has its reflection in our double and the double transmits it to the spiritual body. It is only in this way that spiritual beings can perceive it. Death can also come from the free and unexpected act of another person and this act cannot be predicted, neither by man nor by the gods.

A bird or a flight of birds, of a particular color and flying in a determined direction have been, in some cases, the voluntary heralds of death. This was due to the existing communication between man and the collective soul of a species of birds. The birds are of all animal creatures the most likely of an alliance with men. Once this alliance exists, one can expect of it the capital service of announcing death.

Death is sometimes perceived as the compact and gentle presence of a loved being filling the room of a dying person. It happened to healthy people to have that feeling of a compact and gentle presence. It was the forecast of their death which should only occur a little later. Death had come and then had withdrawn.

The least attractive form of the forecast, although the forecast should always be welcomed with satisfaction, is the view of death in its millennium skeleton aspect, especially if this skeleton has a vague desire of embracing. But it must be considered with wise discernment, because this appearance is the one that has the most chance of being a creation of the imagination.

**

One night, I had the feeling that the hour of my death had come.

We have, sometimes, at night, when we wake up with a start, a decrease of reasonable faculties. We are dominated by a memory, a fear, or the feeling of an illusory presence. And we do not have, for a long time, the ability to find the true proportion of things.

It was a summer night with a moon of which I saw the light from my half opened window. Sitting on my bed, in the awakening unconscious

I had the stupid sensation that death, divine character, was in that light and had the popular skeleton aspect with a scythe under which it is represented in childish images.

I did nothing of what I prescribed myself to do at that capital minute of death. My last thought that I knew so important, I did not steer it towards gods and the spiritual world. My last thought related only to terrestrial things, quite terrestrial. I dressed hastily and came down the hotel stairs quickly, without this activity modifying the certainty of my last hour.

I found myself on a quiet harbor. What time was it? It was of little importance. The most important was to enjoy one last time the beauty of forms that I was about to leave. These forms were splendid and silence impressive. The trees in the square were still as stone trees. Boats, with a solemn slowness, were setting off on the waters. My thought concentrated on the letters I had to write. I had to write to the charming creatures of tender things, insignificant, yet essential. Why it took so long? Full of mercy, the character with the scythe gave me time to write.

But it had to be done without delay. The cafes were closed. All were asleep. I saw prospects of dead alleys. Will the entire world die with me? It was perhaps already. I was the sole survivor of the planet. The letters were then useless. But no, the boats were sailing despite the lack of wind. I had always been intrigued by the movement the sails printed when no breeze stirred the air. This mystery, like many others, would never be revealed.

I began to walk at random. Why death wouldn't be a destructive force likely to take the form that usually the popular imagination lends it. When the force is about to be exercised, the one who feels the strength in him sees the image appear linked to the idea of the force. This image was, in a sense, real. I saw clearly in the moonlight, the character with the scythe. Perhaps had he descended the stairs behind me. Maybe he followed me, smiling at my agitation, and of what smile!

I left the city at a rapid pace. I followed a road, I walked along the pine woods where once stood here and there a sleeping house. How my life had been vain! How I had lost time! But at what would I have better spent that time? To improve myself? Was it not selfishness? To help others? Weren't they locked up in their arrogant shells, unable to host?

The stars were attached to a prodigious height. The beauty was overwhelming. Surely I did not have quite enjoyed during my life. The letters to write seemed to me less urgent. I often wondered the little tub that was someone's death in the depths of hearts. Were the most loved ones were only loved for a little time. I had known a lover possessed of love who had thrown herself screaming in the pit where the coffin of the man she adored had just been descended. Force had to be used to drag her away and she had bitten one of those who were engaged in this task. One week, only one week after, she was dancing in a night restaurant. And similar examples were innumerable. The essence of our loving relationships is without substance.

The dead go fast; it is said to paint this rapid oblivion. They go slowly. Through the dream that surrounds them, they are desperately begging for a loving thought. We run away from them by the icy silence of our soul.

I followed the course of my letters when they were written. I saw the postman drop them among janitors. I witnessed sincere but short emotions. All my farewell powers could not interrupt meal times, those of strolls, to change the ordinary rhythm of life. Moreover, it was good as it was. Have I not say frequently that death was to be a subject of rejoicing as the one who died went to a better state? It is illogical. I wanted to be sure of not being understood, sure to be regretted with the usual manifestations of grief.

And then, I perceived the true power of life and how the proximity of death imposed a self-betrayal. We come back down when dying in the root of ones being, where there are only blind instincts. The superior thoughts that has taken years to hatch are no longer attached to you, they leave you and one goes back again through all forms of his mediocrity until having in oneself only the primary thrust of the seed.

What led me in this moment on this path, was a greed of last enjoyment, the love of clean air, small gardens, fragrant pines. What made me walk fast, was fear, an unacknowledged fear of dying. I wanted to escape with all my reason to what I conceived as beneficial and desirable. And this fear made me see death under the most childish aspects. I was ashamed of myself. I retraced my steps. Slower, by the way.

The boats were far way on the sea. The night seemed to fade. A lean man walked along the harbor carrying on his shoulder a line to fish.

Was it death in a more human aspect, death that was going to settle for a fish?

I went towards my hotel. My normal faculties were almost back. I gave up any letter writing. A newspaper article came to my mind. It recounted the experiences of courageous metaphychists that were caught for analyzing the sensation of death. After coming round, they had told to their colleagues that "when the noose was tense they were dazzled by a bright light and deafened by the noise of thunder." Yet, I only perceived the gray morning fog and the sound of a car trunk, far away, on a road. So I was not overgrown by any warning sign of death. Praise be to the death since it left again!

In my room, I cast a wary glance at the window. There was no more moonlight, skeleton, scythe. So I became sad.

— May my soul be delivered from fear! Shall it not drop the few white pebbles picked up in the desert, the white pebbles of wisdom, in order to escape an image, it has brought forth! May my soul be not afraid of his dreams! Even if the incorruptible goddess, to announce her presence, would take a form of bones, even if she was holding a scythe as a symbol of the destruction of the bodies, we should smile of his presence. Death grants time to those who ask, if they invoke clever pretexts, duties to perform, tasks to complete. May my soul guard itself from requesting a delay! It is necessary to follow death with everything one has loved, without abandoning an idea, without dropping a white stone. The soul must be like a good master who at the time of changing of stay, gathers all his servants so that they accompany him where he is going. What would be thought of the master who would leave behind him a servant because she would have a too beautiful face? May my soul be delivered of fear!

Forecast of everyone's death

Polish scientists have recently studied the case of one of their compatriots who, in the presence of another, can, without error, indicate the day and time of his death. His predictions extend on weeks and are undoubtedly established. His process of knowledge is in the smell. I do not know myself with a similar gift to the one of that Pole with an improved sense of smell. No psychic institute have had to study my supersensible faculties, since I do not have any. Yet I perceive with certainty the death of the society in which I live in.

I cannot say whether it is with the sense of smell that I have this perception, although the bowels of the cities emit by their sewer a monstrous odor of decay. I do hear death walking behind me when I walk through the streets. My perception comes from a sense that I do not realize and which is subtler than smell or hearing.

The knowledge of the ambient death manifested itself first to me by a concern of my nerves and a vague anxiety. Then it turned into compassion for all beings that I saw because I had the feeling of the perishable nature of all that occupied them. I shrugged, seeing the importance they attached to works of which they sketched the beginning and of which they would not see the end. I was often tempted to warn them, but stopped when making it by the poverty of reasons I could give the wrong opinion one would have of me. I finally got used to living in houses of short duration, reading books destined to fall into dust, among the creatures which would not know old age.

I doubted the accuracy of my perception. I wondered if I wasn't considering the problem of death for too long and if it had not determined in me a kind of obsession. I remembered that the occultist Eliphas Levi had told, I do not know in which of his books, only after a thorough study of death, he had fallen into a deep state of melancholy that had almost led him to suicide. He attributed this to the presence of ghosts and wandering larvae which were filling his atmosphere.

One of my friends that I recently met, has told me that for having, in a too continuous way, thought of death, he also had thoughts of suicide, in order to end this fear.

It is not the same for me. No larvae surrounded me with its folds. No ghost—and I regret—comes visit me. I had only once, when I woke up suddenly, the sensation of an impending death and this feeling was a sleep effect and of an unreasoning terror, more than a hunch. While my forecast has an external character. It is provided to me by beings and things that I see and I discern a match between this input and the rhythm of my inner vision.

How will come this death of society? I have no idea. Will it be due to a geological upheaval?

Will it happen after a war which duration and terrible nature will suffice to destroy the existing forms of life? Will there be, as there has been in history, a sudden proliferation of Asian peoples and will these peoples go over Europe and Paris, as they did once over Persia and Baghdad. Will Bolshevism conquer the world and will the transformation it will undergo to it be called destruction? I have not the slightest indication in this regard.

I thought several times that the state of collective anxiety in which men live around me, as a result of new challenges of life, could have communicated me this feeling of everyone's death. But this anxiety would have had been communicated to me without my knowledge, because personally I do not feel it, either through ignorance of its causes, either by natural indifference or by resignation to events.

I noticed that my intuition of a collective death was sharper and had the strength of a certainty, the few times I happened to sit in a dance hall. The dance, at least the conventional dance we dance today, betrays those who volunteer to it. It allows the stupidity of each and its native pretension, usually masked by the attitude or facial expression, to breathe freely. When I noted with sadness what concentration of mediocrity was a dancing room, my sadness was soon accompanied by the feeling that people who were moving before me, had little time to live, at least in this way and that therefore they were right to enjoy their last pleasures. This feeling was confirmed to me by all their movements. Each dancer seemed to know that the band was going to be interrupted by a tocsin of death. I witnessed a strange funeral ball.

I must say, to be honest, that not long ago, I had a similar feeling, when one of my friends was leaving for America. I was tempted to divert this trip, assuring him that disasters which would shortly occur would prevent him from returning to France. I did nothing, thinking that my forecast was based on too fragile foundations. How I was right! My friend went and returned safely, having made profitable business and the only disaster that occurred had no global character and was a serious illness of which I suffered.

But this only partially diminishes the value of my forecast. It remains for me a fact and a fact that is renewed. This is not an argument against it that months have passed without any forewarning of death has occurred. Forecasts cannot measure time. If an isolated individual emits an odor of death, which can be felt by a Pole a few weeks before, this should be a few years before a company that includes a host of individuals testifies, in its atmosphere, the foretaste of its end.

If we examine in particular the flesh of a creature, we see no mottled shade indicating decomposition. If we consider the compact stones that constitutes the backbone of a church, we find them solid, united by cement, full of cohesion. The elevators ascend hotels regularly, trains run on their tracks, people go about their business, life is in its apparent fullness. But there is perhaps a secret discouragement, a decrease of ardor, an indoor weariness, as if a warning had been given to all souls, without them noticing it. And perhaps it is this watchword without syllables that I perceived.

It should be noted, moreover, that I am not alone in predicting a future disaster. A British astrologer announced the invasion by the sea, of all northern Europe, and the collapse of a large part of England under water. The year 1933 is called the year of fire by a group that was formed in Paris for the purpose of spiritual assistance at the time of the terrible material crisis that will pass through humanity. Other astrologers and other seers agree to affirm that this date will mark, for men of the West, a formidable turn. Of course, all these annunciations can be only modern branches of that great tree of terror which is mounted through the ages and has always spawns an expectation of world's end whose perfume should be a need of human nature, since so many people get intoxicated by it.

I personally believe that the destruction of our society, such as the destruction of all that rots by continuing to live, would be a great good for the good and virtuous men who belong to it. The expression of the current human effort is the machine. However, the machine turns into ugliness all that is beautiful. The essence of all desire is wealth. Yet wealth is a symbol of matter and enjoyment. The momentum of the society is retrograde and drives them despite those who kept in their heart a fragment of spiritual hope. Goodness and virtue can only express themselves imperfectly in ugliness and evil. The attraction of ugliness and evil is powerful because it is exercised with familiar objects, the small pleasures of daily life.

Those who deserve not to be lost, risk to lose themselves without thinking about it.

In fact, when one has not reached an advanced stage of development one should be well advised to frequently change body. The grain of perfection which is harvested in each life is mostly harvested during youth. Men quickly freeze as part of their situation and their families. They take their interests and the interests of their relatives to a noble ideal. Rare are those who, by getting older, glimpse the truth and cultivate it. The more one frequently and the more he has chances of finding the incarnation where the light will appear.

And, how not to think without shuddering for hope at a time when the roads will be conducted without being disturbed by automobile passages, where engines will perish under the rust, where wireless devices will drop their arms in heavens, where dead airplanes will no longer tear azure, where forests will begin to grow again, where men fleeing the turmoil they have unleashed, will seek shelter under trees and in the rocks and perhaps will find there again the wisdom they have lost!

It is in the aftermaths of a great pain that an individual gets into himself, changes his life, become better. Thus a collective disaster will be for all a vast way of purification.

May the signs of destruction be truthful, astrologers have calculated well, seers have seen right, my humble intuition have sensed accurately!

The choice

Long before the minute of one's death, a choice must be made, a choice of a great importance which must be made in a human state and determines endless series of consequences. One must have done it before the minutes of his death because this minute can occur suddenly and then one has only the possibility to cease hastily two or three ideas. These ideas must, naturally, have been made sparkling since a long time in order to be visible despite the precipitation and the darkness.

We had to make an irrevocable choice between two currents that guide the human souls, between the current of love and that of selfishness, between good and evil.

Primitive Buddhism says, that apart from the inferior forms and the man's form, we have the possibility to reincarnate either in the form of Deva, either in that of Asura. The Asura is the being who, having tasting the pleasures of selfishness, wants to perpetuate them. He wants to fortify more and more his personality, make it enjoy more as a separated organism. He aspires to a much more distinctive life. He delays as much as he can the movement towards the unity of the mind. The Deva, on the contrary, has ceased, during his passage in the human state, the natural orientation of the world. He knows that the law pushes all creatures, by the expansion of love, towards the unity of the mind.

The man must choose between those two divergent currents. The force of expansion is good; the force of condensation or selfishness is evil. Evil is only the resulting of the effort accomplished by all the beings who do not want to resign themselves to obey the spiritual force of the world, and persist to remain in the current of materialization.

The error is understandable. It seems that nature wanted to make light of his creatures. For countless ages, the law has been for these creatures, to become more perfect in the material order, to acquire more and more complicated organs where can express souls more and more personal.

But at a certain level of achievement, the law changes. The current is spiritualized. Beings have conquered their personality only to abdicate. After having aspired to separation and pursuing the ruthless battle of the struggle for life, they must aspire to unity through love. Those who are rebellious to this law are those who opted for evil, for the duration of the being they have created through countless passages of incarnations.

Most men have passed life without knowing the problem. They have been divided between currents of altruism and currents of selfishness. But some have measured the happiness or the misfortune than one could attain by following the cosmic law or by entering into conflict against it, and they have chosen the excessive development or their personalities. Yet, the human will can to some extent upset the force of the cosmic law. These men who have cultivated the magic of the will often lead an ascetic life and have renounced to social ambitions along with the sage and saints who follow the divine path. They are neither perverts, nor bad ones in the common meaning of the word. They would not commit evil for evil. But, their inner principle being the suppression of love, they would destroy without any pity, all those who would be opposed to their development.

Those perfect proud, those conscious selfish, although quite numerous are difficult to recognize in life. We see only the multitude of their unconscious imitators. Currently all men act as if they had, deliberately, opted for evil. It seems that a foolish watchword has flowed across the planet. Everyone tries to destroy in oneself, the expansive power of love.

This will probably only increase. Its reason is easy to understand. Since the beginning of the world, many men have known that the wisdom was to escape incarnation and they have learned the methods that would allow them to stop entering the form of man, subject to pain. In this way best ones leave earth forever. If these pure hearts, that elevated towards divine love would have come back, we would find them and we would notice a sensitive improvement of humanity. But we do not find them. On the contrary, those who have developed virtues of material order, virtues engendered by the taste of enjoyment and well being, are more numerous than in olden days. Likewise, remarkable men speaking of physical courage are increasing and these men have a more and more important place, they are more and more admired. We find more heroes ready to make the sacrifice of their lives for the family, for the society, for the country, that is to say for interests having a common character. It means that they reincarnate all the more quickly, being all the more chained to the group for which they have sacrificed.

On the contrary, spiritual heroes do not return to us, or if they do, it is in a quite exceptional way. Also humanity, deprived of higher examples of love, becomes increasingly material, and this materialization will only worsen.

The choice by spiritual path, the paths of gods is all the more urgent. It will be more and more difficult. A time will probably come when the two paths will not be able to distinguish themselves, where they will be only one, that of selfishness, and where the other will appear as a dangerous aberration that the societies will feel obliged to punish.

The choice must be made unequivocally and with a sincere heart. It contains an alliance with the Devas with whom we dream to unite and a renouncement to the part of oneself whose aspirations are terrestrial. This renouncement seems at first very painful because we think we are giving up a priceless treasure. We need to know ourselves well enough to know what we are giving up.

Know thyself

"Know thyself", says the wisdom of ancient Greeks.

When a pilgrim, in hope of discovering the truth, arrived at Delphi and presented himself in the threshold of the temple, he was taken in front of the most ancient priests of Apollo. This one looked at him squarely in the face. If he recognized in him an ordinary searcher of truth, he would ask him offerings, made him bow in front of statues or breath exhalations of sacred herbs. But if he saw in his look the light of intelligence he contented himself by showing him the engraved inscription on the pediment of the temple: Know thyself. And if the pilgrim understood, and if by taking back his stick, was about to go away, the old priest would bow in front of him and kiss his sandals.

This last case must have been infinitely rare. It seems to me that if I went from Toulouse towards Delphes to learn wisdom, even if I had been stroke by illumination in front of the formulation: Know thyself! I would not have left silently, I would have liked to see the temple which splendor was great, contemplate the pure forms of statues, taste the intoxication of sacred herbs, and even if I could, ask a question to the Pythia, a question of which I would knew the answer, to assure myself by ruse of its true character. It is only after, sitting alone in the countryside, that I would have meditated on the essential word.

Thus we must do. One has to look at the statues and even touch them to know if they are made of solid marble, or of stucco, hollow inside. One must intoxicate by the herbs of the earth, especially if they are prepared by men appointed to the temple because they allow certain spiritual elevations that one only obtains thanks to the genius of plants. One must question the oracle, because there is a lesson either in his lie, either in his truth. After that it is necessary to look inside oneself.

The first gesture of the one who wants to know himself is to look at oneself in a mirror. It is a great lesson. It is necessary to look with the position to see oneself in it and for that to look long enough. When I have experienced this, I saw a man with hair much more grey than those I supposed myself. These hairs fell limply, as if they regretted their lost vitality. It was poor hair. I saw eyes strangely starring of which one had less brilliance than the other, eyes deprives of this beautiful certainty that we see in the eyes of men who never think. I saw an affected smile of which the voluntary irony was hiding the distress.

And behind this figure much older than I had thought, there was another one who appeared, though a steam, as his unconscious double. This one was charming, but so young! His hair was long and solid and had a romantic haircut. His glance was sparkling and full of childish faith. There was in his amazed smile the joy of success. From his face already sculpted by desire, emanated the trust in the goodness of men and the love of life.

What has this old young man become, with his taste for poetry, women and something confusing to which he gave to the little happiness the name of ideal? He has disappeared. It was perhaps the best of all beings of which I had successively the form. And what became those who have preceded and followed him? The child that I was is dead. The young man that I was is dead. The mature man that I am will die in its turn by the last transformation of old age. Only this contour remains, in this steam, at the bottom of the mirror. All creatures that I have been, took their places in a succession of ghosts of which I summarizes the lost chain.

Know thyself! By what am I different from the others? By what special flaws, by what tiny qualities of which the nuances make my own color?

I am someone who likes to hear the sound of his footsteps on a deserted road, when the evening is golden and the land is aromatic. But the path must be in a very limited region, at the south of France, between the mountains of the Moors and the Mediterranean.

I am someone who likes to lie down on a carpet, an Arabic carpet preferably, looking the smoke from his cigarette turn and inventing beautiful faces that do not exist.

I am someone who likes to caress the neck of a woman who dreams, because of the mysterious warmth of life that emerges from it.

I am someone who likes to read books where are recounted long journeys and dangerous adventures in countries where I will never go.

I am someone who regrets not having met a dog, smart among dogs or another animal friend with the man, like the snake or the elephant, which would have shown him that loyal friendship of which only animals are capable of.

I am someone that beauty, female bodies, trees that rise, certain arrangements of words touches.

I am someone who would like to understand why the universe exists, why man is born and why he dies.

I am someone who could never lose his first faculty of astonishment, who has crossed life, surprised, and who will die probably surprised.

And after that? What else am I? Almost nothing else.

The abyss of doubt

— Oh my God! Why have you abandoned me?

There is no more terrible word. If the one who had been after the Buddha one of the most perfect men that humanity has known, has doubted, felt abandoned, at the time when he was quite close of death, means that he had no absolute certainty. The ordeal of the cross, despite the blood of the hands and feet, allowed the tortured one to survive three days in agony. It seems that death came for Jesus after three hours. He was then going to reach that realm of the Father he has promised so many times to the chosen ones, this Father's realm which is the Buddhists Nirvana. He should have already glimpsed it. Whatever the torment of the flesh, he should have been elated by the proximity of the divine state. And he exclaimed: Why have you abandoned me?

Confucius and the Buddha have also exhorted those who believed in their science not to take care of what would happen after their death. Had they therefore no certainty? Did they consider a possibility that their belief came to betray them? Socrates, according to Apologia, said to his judges: "Either death is the entire destruction or it is the passage in another place". Thus he did not consider the hypothesis or destruction as impossible. He examined it as seriously as that of the immortality of the soul!

Philosophers who have looked all their lives at the problem of death, as Epicurus, as Zeno and their disciples, did not believe in the future life. Lucretius has affirmed that the soul intimately linked to the body was mortal as him." When I will be no more, all feeling will have died in me", said Cicero. "Death consumes us and leaves nothing to remain of us", says Seneca. "There is no little boy nor old woman stupid enough to believe of what is told about another life", says Juvenal. According to Petrarch, this is what is believed in Avignon in the papal entourage: "The future world, the last judgment, hell's punishments, joys of para-

dise are called absurd and childish fables". "We can make many con-
jectures to our advantage and have high hopes, but have no certainty",
says Descartes.

And the epitaphs that we read on the stones found attest that private
individuals, who were not philosophers, nor poets, have doubted in all
times and doubted with enough strength to want their doubt be engraved on the gravestones.

"In the Hades, says one, we find neither Charon, nor Aeacus, nor
Cerberus. All of us that death sends there, we are only bones and ashes".

"Dead for eternity, says another one, I will neither say my name, nor
my father, nor my actions. I am a little ash, nothing more, and will never
be something else. My fate awaits you."

"The Amenti is the country of the heavy sleep and darkness, mourn-
ing stay for those who live there."

Thereby doubt appeared of all times and has occupied the same place
as faith. A crow of men has looked sincerely what they were in reality.
They have recognized that there were so little that it was impossible
that this little will eternal. They have thought that death was an act of
definitive destruction.

Doubt has the form of an abyss. The soul, when it presents itself to
it, sees suddenly a depth that is lost in the darkness. But it is not itself
that falls in an unexpected night. It is the animated beings to which
we have lend a divine life, the beautiful ideas on which we relayed as
on young women's shoulders. We see erase everything that was dear to
you, there is nothing left, and we stay in a desperate solitude, in front
of a nothingness that terrifies you without destroying you.

I sometimes stood above the abyss. I had not gone to him. It had dug
under my footsteps. I only had the time to perceive its darkness and it
has disappeared.

There are people less fortunate who have it constantly before them.
They do not fall into it though. They remain cheerful and content with
life, despite the proximity of this abyss.

But all doubts of the earth prove nothing. It is normal that a man made
of matter, who only sees matter, only attributes reality to the material

proof. With a mysterious and scholarly dexterity, nature arranged for a triple veil covers the existence of the future life. It has wanted the secret to be as a bonus to a certain quality of wisdom. Each has in his spiritual conformation a faculty to believe or not to believe which is outside intelligence. But each can acquire the faculty to believe that he does not have. Each can retreat, then remove the emergence of the abyss. He must not do it by the method of stupidity prescribed by Pascal, by the holy water, by the blind obedience to rites and by saying: "What I am risking?"

There is no mystery that we have to believe and that we have not. The Buddha recommended to his disciples to believe nothing, even his own words, if their minds did not recognize as valid what he said.

The abyss of faith is as deep and more formidable as that of doubt, because it is more attractive. From it emanates a perfume, which has a lingering odor of church, but which invites to a blissful sleep where the thought no longer has any part.

The epithet of blind of which one have often made follow the word faith is significant. One does not see in that abyss and if one sings hymns, one does not know its meaning.

Besides the abyss of doubt and the abyss of faith merge to a certain depth. It is enough to go down very far.

The one who by the narrow path of meditation sinks in the backwaters of the soul where there are no more currents, in the silent stretches where the sun of the earth is nothing but a frozen reflection, glimpses a temple with immortal columns, that draws its light from its own substance. It is the temple of certainty where thoughts of every wine shine as bunk crystals, where every man who doubts has traced a sign with his tears. Its geometry is perfect as the laws of the world. All the figures of gods are inscribed in its architectures. He rests in the immeasurable depths of the soul and as fantastic corals of the underwater world; the primordial truths grow around him. He is perfect as the number, harmonious as music, radiant as the proved truth. He stands immobile in the darkness of interior oceans.

The secret sister

Each of us lives side by side with a sister with a divine face, a secret sister whose smile he does not know, whose dress he has not touched, whose existence he does not know. We may be comforted by her when we suffer. We could be cured from the suffering of solitude, through her presence. But we do not know that she is here. This sister is the part of our soul that remains hidden.

Nature has wanted that a portion of the universe remains invisible to us. We only perceive with our senses the physical matter. But there are subtler plans of existence that we do not know. Similarly, we know of our soul only the weak fragment illuminated by consciousness. Man has perhaps no other way to perfect himself than to learn to see what is invisible.

It is necessary to discover the face of divine sister. When we have discovered it once by a wonderful experience, we are so happy with this discovery, that doubt dies of itself and that death becomes what is most desirable. For death leads us to the identification with our hidden soul. But for this identification is conscious in the afterlife, so that it has full effect, it is necessary that the experience has been carried out previously in the world of causes, that is to say, in our lifetime.

To discover ones soul, the eternal sister, the saints, the mystics or mere philosophers have indicated a thousand methods of meditation. All are as ineffective as the last? A method is only valid for the one who has found it. The prayer addressed with fervor to any God is a preparation for the discovery of the soul. But the one who prays without exactly knowing the purpose can only attain a drying of the heart by the lack of results. The ignorant who eternally prays, only prepare himself eternally. He sometimes takes the means for the end. He can sometimes be led towards the opposite path by his own exaltation. Some favored men attain immediately to the experience, as if they were affected by a special grace. The poet Tennyson said that he obtained it, almost at will, by repeating for a few minutes the syllables of his name. Plotinus, having scrutinized throughout his entire life problems of the origin of things and of the future life, he only achieved it three times. Many Hindu mystics, many Catholic saints, had to reach by ecstasy the divine knowledge and they have told it to nobody.

The feature of the experiment is that it makes us feel that we are eternal by the link that unites us to the divine soul: yet, perhaps are eternal only souls who know they are eternal. Perhaps that the others determine their own destruction by their ignorance and their denial.

But how to manage to make the experience that gives joy, the liberating experience? If there is a special grace, how to acquire it? I feel it would be pointless for me to repeat the syllables of my name. It is a strange method which should be valid only for the poet Tennyson. Should we wait until some Deva comes, of friendship, whisper words softly, or trace an indicating sign, among the darkness of the dream? I often thought I was a Deva's friend. I heard veiled words, confusingly distinguished of the signs. But there is no true formula but the one we find, of sure science but the one we learn by reading about its inner book.

Vivekananda advises, to achieve the highest human state, to imagine a golden lotus placed a few centimeters from ones head and fix through meditation ones thought on him. He also advises to represent oneself a flame that burns instead of the heart thinking that this flame is your own soul. In this flame, there will be a more dazzling flame, which will be the core of your soul, its divine essence. I changed in the sense of my ideal habits, the indication of Vivekananda and I replaced the dazzling flame by the perfect face of the unknown sister. For the one who, during his life, has placed the greatest beauty in a woman's face have to use his old dreams to reach the highest dream.

There was a time when I believed that it was necessary to live in a hermitage, to break with his way of life and to call in solitude the coming of ecstasy. I think now that the truth must be able to slip in any place, in the middle of the most vulgar men, among the daily activities. I resolved myself to change nothing of the habits of my ordinary life. I placed in my heart the divine face and it accompanies me all day long.

When I go home, when I put down my hat, and I sit in the evening, without thinking of anything, I feel he is a little more specific and I guess his delicious features, his eyes fixed upon me with an inexpressible sweetness. I noticed that when I had a cause of grief, the face was more beautiful face, the eyes had a deeper light. They veiled slightly on the contrary if I felt joy of having a coarse cause. I concluded that there was an intimate relationship between the inner beauty of the soul and the pain and that the quality of the joy draws away or closer by the variation of its shades the presence of the divine sister.

Perhaps will I need to experience great pain to identify myself with the divine soul and be aware of my eternity. It is not impossible that a great joy of love brings me to the same result. Each carries in oneself a herald knowledge of the general meaning of one's life. I know that if I had given in to the human need to personify my aspirations, it is because I have to get closer to the divine through the contemplation of beauty.

The sister whose face appeared in my heart, holds an ivory wand around which is enrolled a golden snake. She has blue eyes like Pallas Athena, but she has neither her large size nor his thick ankles, and mostly neither his helmet. She is of a medium size, she smiles because she is by no means austere, enthusiasm is her dominant quality. She is called beauty, but also intelligence and wisdom.

A day will come when she will stand next to me. This will be the day when I have understood the beauty of the world, the need and urgency of death by which we approach this beauty of which the source is spirit. Perhaps it will be during a dinner and I will suddenly cease to have an unreasonable contempt for my fellow. Instead of seeing around me peacocks dressed in black, birds of prey hiding under their nails under polished boots, pigs with colored ties, I will see pitiful brothers trying to escape the chains of animalism. It will maybe happen in a bus. The anonymous faces will cease to be silent and closed in front of me. They will let shine living and familiar souls. Perhaps it will be among the books of my room. All the thoughts trapped under the million characters of pages will become animated realities. I will feel one with the eternal movement of the mind. The furniture, the city and the space will appear to me as the reflections of a subtler primary cause. By an expansion full of joy where my consciousness will be by no mean annihilated, I will go from one end to the other of the universe, penetrating all things, the smallest as the biggest with the ease of love.

I will do this experiment due to the realized notion of what was for me beauty. I understand then why this beauty is also called intelligence, why it is also called wisdom and that her name is also death.

And I will finally penetrate the meaning of the admirable word of the Zohar: "Death is the kiss of God".

Prayer for those who call death

Not everyone fears death. There are some who call it with an ardor as deep as secret. They do not let reflect it. They accomplish the rites of life, go to offices, shake their friends hand, sit at family tables. They have ordinary and indifferent faces. Yet, they wait and they have hope in death. A shyness retains them. They dare not violate destiny. In the middle of the visible disorder of nature, they are afraid to be a slur on a mysterious order where they have their places. And then, they remember the curses they heard during their childhood, the catechisms words, the threat of reasonable men. And they support the sadness of life.

My God! At this hour of the night, there are beings who have no friendship and no love and who only expect from death a fraternity they have always asked and have never received.

I think of those souls who have had hunger for goodness and who have had thirst for justice and who have never been satiated.

I think of those lovers who have given themselves with all their gift power, who have been abandoned and do not know how to destroy a body stripped of pleasure and judged unlovable.

I think of those arrogant who have never opened up to anyone, who have confined themselves in their solitude and of whom, only death could tear their seal of silence off.

I think of those who have looked for God and who have not found him, to those who have called and to whom no answer has been made and who think they will hear the answer and will see God beside them, when death will come.

I think of these poor families that go on rivers banks and watch the water pass, water where more courageous deceased slowly descend, stripped of the burden of misery.

I think of all the girls of pain called ladies of the night. Of all men who were born without means of defense in the middle of the race of wolves. Of all God's creatures who are the creatures of hell.

I think of all those who have neither had the bread made with corn nor the bread made with the mind, neither the wine made with grapes, nor the wine made with the dream and who would have preferred death to the work without rest and to the rest without joy.

Shorten their sufferings, oh rapid! Come comfort them, oh gentle! Set yourself on their chest, oh light! You alone give the bread to the hungry, the wine to the dreamy, the affection to the one who is without brother.

Why are you not answering to the salutations? What is that date that you arbitrarily fix, always too close or always too distant? Are you yourself submissive to a higher power or is it the man who, by his actions, has mysteriously fixed his destiny?

The human body is fragile and ugly and even so it is very difficult to destroy it! An inner majesty and a strange possibility of pain, hidden in his blood, stops the arm of the one who wants to hit himself. But how many are there, oh death! Who would bless you, if you stopped, without consulting them, the steady coming and going of their breath?

Open them the door, oh liberator! It is the weakest and the best who put their hope in you. These are the ones that a native nobility prevents to commit evil, those who have conceived a too high idea of the beauty of souls. Show them the real beauty of life, oh divine!

The vow

It is at the minute of death that it is necessary to possess the greatest joy of life. May this word be present for me, when will come for me the little twilight morning when ordinarily leave the dying ones. The molecules of my organism will be mysteriously disintegrated. But no resonance will warn me that the judgment of my life is set in the secret clock that beats in my heart. May I have one minute to clearly remember the word and turn it into light!

I know that the road unknown to the deceased is directed towards the rising sun. I know that there is a youth of the other life. Here we are younger and more beautiful because the form is clothed in the purity of his soul. May I rush myself towards this youth with the joy of owning, without deviating from my path for a possible farewell, for a last kiss that no lip would moisten!

I know that the road known to the deceased is directed towards the dark earth. My body will go to a small cemetery that I chose, on top of a hill among friendly pines, not far from the sea. He will undergo terrestrial transformations in the middle of hot stones and illuminated beasts. My soul will go towards the rising sun.

That then, those for whom I was little truthful forgive me! That those who I have stripped of a pleasure forgive me! May forgive me those who made me suffer with their ugliness, those whose ignorance seemed greater than mine! May I get away with the friendship of the living and the good reception of the dead!

I know that the desire of beauty, the artistic impulses, the self-giving, are qualities that have their development only with the expansion of the soul produced by death. May I give myself in joy, by hugging what has no bounds!

But I do not consent to lose what has been my human treasure. Each guards what he incorporates to it. You who have loved me throughout my life, who have smiled at me with loving faces, I take your eternal images as the luggage of the imperfect man that I was. You are few, but whatever the number! I am happy of my part of love. I will look at you while walking and I will see you regardless of the density of cosmic darkness accumulated around me. I know that beings change, that beings forget. I will prevent you from forgetting me by recreating you with my true thoughts.

And I am making as of now a vow and by hammering it with my memory, by consolidating it with my desire, I am making look like an arrow of soul, as bright as a star, as gifted with wings as a celestial bird. So that this vow precedes me as a guide, carrying to the unknown powers my annunciation.

A time will perhaps come when I will be against my will precipitate in the incarnation. If there is a possibility of escaping this fall, I will keep myself strongly attached to it, like a man on a mast in a sea storm, and I will open my arms to attract to me those that I love. But if I am carried away by irresistible currents, if the defining laws push me, if I am called by the winds that rise of bones, if, through the millions of seeds, I am too blind to see, kneaded by a substance too compact to feel, I vow to be thrown among the companions of the current life where I still write these lines!

I vow to find those who have made me suffer and those who have loved me, carrying their burden of evil and their disappointed hopes for me to lighten them from the burden with my new courage, that I deluge their hopes with the small drop of wisdom that I could snatch from the shadows!

I vow to be born of the same father and same mother, even if they are in the most miserable condition.

This misery will not be misery for me, if I share it with them. Every childhood is painful by the hardness of the earth, the indifference of all, the limit of the consciousness. Whether it is them who give me warm, the bread and the thought! That they do not hold it against me if I have not thought about them after their death! That they do not reject me as an ungrateful. That they pronounce three times at dawn the syllables of my future name so that I break out of the world of larvae! That in the prepared cradle, they receive me with my dark thoughts, my worried curiosities and my imperishable enthusiasm! That they put on my lips the morsel of salt, that accustoms to the salt of tears!

As I choose them at the time of departure, that they choose me at the time of return!

THE END